Exploring
the
Insect
World

Exploring
the
Insect World

by
Margaret J. Anderson

McGraw-Hill Book Company
NEW YORK   ST. LOUIS   SAN FRANCISCO   DÜSSELDORF
JOHANNESBURG   KUALA LUMPUR   LONDON   MEXICO
MONTREAL   NEW DELHI   PANAMA   RIO DE JANEIRO
SINGAPORE   SYDNEY   TORONTO

Pictures appearing on pages 29, 32, 41, 43, 51, 52, 60, 61, 62, 65, 66, 67, 105, 107, 108, 113, 122, 123, 124, 127, 132, 133, 135
Courtesy of Margaret J. Anderson.

Picture appearing on page 47
Courtesy of William Bradshaw.

Pictures appearing on pages 15, 94, 149, 150, 154, 155
Courtesy of the Entomology Department, Oregon State University, Corvallis.

Picture appearing on page 143
Courtesy of the United States Department of Agriculture. Photograph by Murray Lemmon.

830625

Library of Congress Cataloging in Publication Data

Anderson, Margaret J
  Exploring the insect world.

  SUMMARY: Experiments and projects reveal the physical characteristics and behavior of a variety of insects.
  1. Insects—Juvenile literature. 2. Insects—Collection and preservation—Juvenile literature.
  [1. Insects] I. Title.
  QL467.2.A52   595.7   73-17412
  ISBN 0-07-001625-9 (lib. bdg.)

Copyright © 1974 by Margaret J. Anderson. All Rights Reserved. Printed in the United States of America. No part of this publication may be reproduced, stored in a retrieval system, or transmitted, in any form or by any means, electronic, mechanical, photocopying, recording, or otherwise, without the written permission of the publisher.

23456789   BPBP   798765

Contents

	Preface	7
1	Insects Everywhere	9
2	Insects Close Up	18
3	Insects on the Night Shift	27
4	Plants and the Insects They Need	37
5	The Hungry Horde	49
6	Galls—Homes Made to Order	59
7	The Silk Spinners	70
8	The Insect Hunters	77
9	The House Builders—Bees and Wasps	87
10	The City Builders—Ants	98
11	Exploring a Pond	111
12	Dragonflies on Patrol	121
13	The Case of the Caddisfly	131
14	Man's Insect Enemies	140
15	Man's Insect Friends	148
	Bibliography	156
	Index	157

TO *Norman*

Preface

MOST PEOPLE either ignore insects or dislike them. Few people realize we couldn't get along without them.

In writing this book, I hope to encourage you to go out and look for insects and make your own discoveries about them. There are no other animals so easy to study, yet so varied. There is a wealth of information on the subject; yet, there is so much to learn. Although scientists have named some 800,000 kinds, or *species,* there are more waiting to be found. Perhaps by you.

You will find a cast of characters in the insect world that equals any Western. There are the "bad guys," such as locusts, that can lay bare a field of grain in an afternoon. There are heroes—the ladybugs that saved the citrus industry. There are the burying beetle "undertakers" that dispose of dead animals, and there is a host of garbage collectors. There are insects that we enjoy simply because they are beautiful, for example, the dancing swallowtail butterfly and the swift, metallic dragonfly.

A man who studies insects is called an *entomologist*. There are far too many species of insects for any one man to know them all. So the entomologist may study the insects that damage our crops, or he may be interested in insects that eat other insects, or he may specialize in insects that carry disease. He may be interested in new species of a particular group of insects. But whatever aspect of insects he studies, he is concerned with how the insect fits into its world.

Some entomologists have expensive equipment— electron microscopes, radiation machines, artificial streams, and so on. But many questions can be answered and experiments performed with no more equipment than you find in your own kitchen.

So I hope this book will help you to go out and really look at insects and find out about their ways. If you investigate carefully and record your observations, then *you* are an entomologist. Wherever you live, insects are waiting. You will find them in city parks, vacant lots, ponds, woods, and fields, and in your own back yard.

CHAPTER 1

Insects Everywhere

YOU FIND insects everywhere. Moths circle the porch light, wasps buzz round the picnic table, fleas bother the dog. There are insects in ponds, in trees, in the soil, and in the basement. One kind of insect lives in the snow on mountaintops and another spends its life in the total darkness of an underground cave. Insects are everywhere.

There are more kinds of insects than all the other kinds of animals. If you doubt this, next time you go on a picnic, count the kinds of animals you see. You may see dogs, cows, squirrels, and several kinds of birds. If you are lucky, you might see deer, frogs, and a snake. Flies, wasps, ants, and mosquitoes will undoubtedly find *you,* and the list of insects will be much longer when you do the looking.

Insect beginnings

Let us travel back through time, back 300 million years. We find ourselves in a strange forest, inhabited by weird creatures. The climate is mild and moist, the ground swampy. The trees of the forest are giant club mosses, horsetails and ferns. Sunning itself by the edge of a swamp is a huge, amphibian creature, about 8 feet long, called *Eryops*. It looks rather like a great, overgrown frog with a tail, and it breaks the silence of the forest with a hoarse croak.

Then, a cockroach scuttles over the damp ground —at least it is something familiar! Gliding through the trees is a creature you recognize but can scarcely believe. It is a giant dragonfly with wings about 30 inches across. Another dragonfly just like it lies dead on the mud.

Another journey—this time to the world of 50 million years ago—finds us again in a land of incredible animals. The great dinosaurs are all gone but a grotesque rhinoceros called *Uintatherium* lumbers down to the river to drink. It has three pairs of blunt horns and a pair of tusks as well. And are those tiny animals at the edge of the wood really horses? They are no bigger than small dogs. Then, in this alien world, we hear a cricket chirp on a leaf, and an ant runs up the trunk of an evergreen tree. The unwary ant gets caught in a drop of sticky resin and cannot get free.

Back in our present world, Eryops is long gone and the first mammals are nothing but fossil bones. But the cockroach still scuttles over the damp ground, the cricket chirps in the grass, and the busy ant runs up the trunk of a tree.

The dragonfly that lay dead in the mud and the

ant that was caught in the resin are our clues to these insects of the past. They have been preserved as fossils in coal and amber. From these fossils, we know that insects were among the earliest land animals and were the first animals to fly in the air.

What is it about insects that has helped them survive so long? What has enabled them to cover so much of the earth?

What is an insect?

Take a close look at an insect such as a grasshopper or a big fly. You will find that it has a hard, shell-like skin. It carries its skeleton on the outside—an exoskeleton. Even the most delicate butterfly has this tough exoskeleton. Animals such as this belong to a large group called *arthropods*. Arthropods include centipedes, millipedes, spiders, crabs, and shrimps, as well as insects.

An adult insect can be separated from all other arthropods by several features. Check over your insect, and make sure that it is one. It is an insect if:

Its body is divided into three parts (head, thorax, and abdomen).
It has three pairs of legs.
It has one pair of antennae (feelers).
It has wings. Most insects have wings. No other arthropods can fly.

You will notice that these features are for adult insects. You will soon find that young insects are too

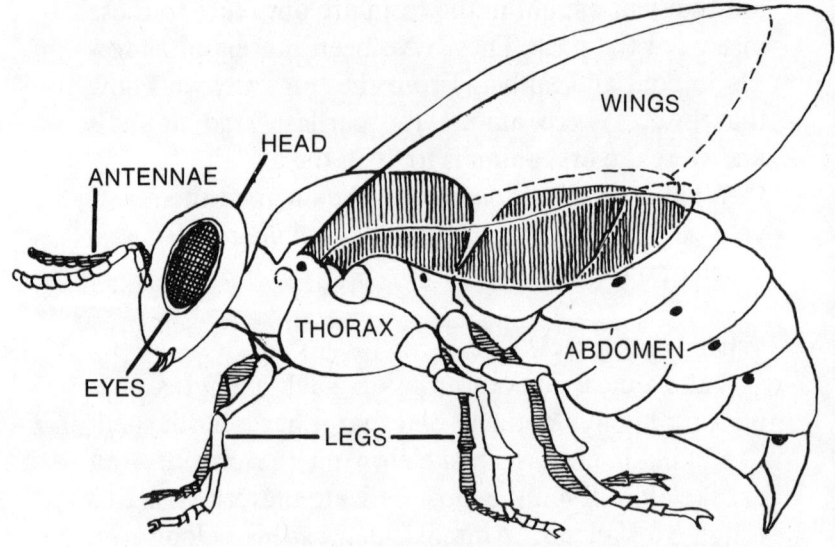

A close-up of an insect showing outer anatomy.

varied to fit any set of rules. The best way to learn about them is by doing a bit of detective work—by rearing them.

The exoskeleton

The hard exoskeleton is one of the keys to the insect's success story. Back in the fifteenth century fighting men were outfitted with suits of armor not unlike an exoskeleton. These consisted of stiff plates separated by movable areas at the joints. They were good protection, but they were heavy. It was hard to breathe through the face mask, or visor, and there was no way for the body heat to escape. How then does the insect manage?

The insect in armor has an advantage over the man in armor because the muscles are attached to the armor itself. There is a very big area for muscle attachment so insects are very strong. If you could jump as well as a grasshopper, then for your height, you would be able to leap half the length of a football field!

The skeleton is made of nonliving material formed by the outer layers of cells of the body. It is a mixture of chemicals. Two important ones are *chitin* and *sclerotin*. These make the skeleton very strong. Even chemicals such as acid and bleach will not dissolve the skeleton.

The exoskeleton has been adapted in different ways that are useful to the insect. The pincer jaws of a soldier ant, the thin, delicate wings of a dragonfly, and the stinger of a bee are all modifications of the skeleton.

How insects breathe

A thin, waxy layer on the surface of the exoskeleton protects and keeps the insect's body from drying out. Without this type of covering the insect would be restricted to moist places like an earthworm. But this waxy layer prevents the insect from breathing through its skin.

Suppose you held a grasshopper's head under water. How long would it take to drown? You would be surprised to find the grasshopper still struggling after 10 minutes, or longer. The reason is that an insect does not breathe through a "nose" on its head;

so, with only its head under water, it would not drown.

A system of small tubes, or *trachea,* carries the air directly to all parts of the animal. The trachea open to the outside through little holes called *spiracles.*

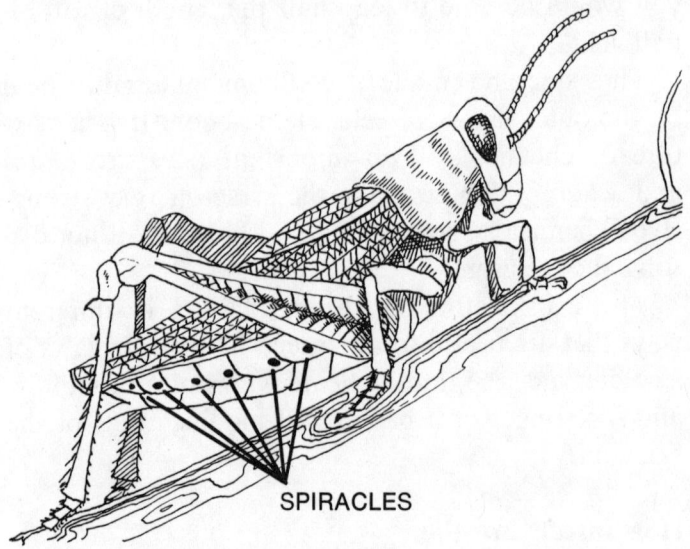

A grasshopper, showing spiracles.

See if you can find the spiracles along the sides of the abdomen of a grasshopper. The number of spiracles varies with different kinds of insects. Some have only one pair.

How insects grow

Another problem connected with the rigid exoskeleton is that, because it is nonliving material, it cannot grow. How does a young insect get bigger? It grows a new skin under the old one and then breaks out of the tight exoskeleton. The new skin is at first soft and elastic and adapts to increases in size and changes in shape, and then becomes hard and protective. This process is called *molting*.

Because an insect grows in this way, there is a limit to the size it can become. In spite of science fiction, you will never meet an ant as big as you are or be attacked by a 100-pound bee. In the vital time during molting, the new, soft skin just cannot support a large body. The biggest insects either have the huge wingspan of some moths, or very long, slender bodies such as the stick insects of the tropics.

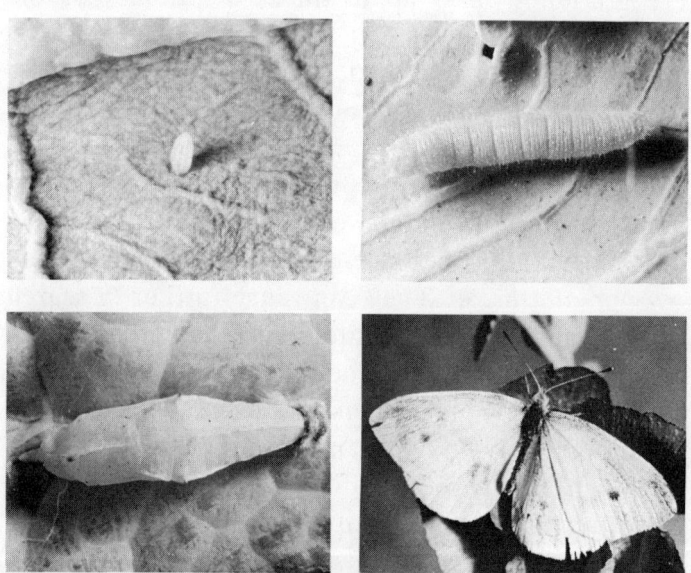

The life story of the Cabbage White butterfly: egg, caterpillar, pupa and adult.

The adult stage of many insects is quite different from the young stage. This change is called *metamorphosis,* which comes from Greek words meaning "change of shape." When you compare a caterpillar with a butterfly, you will agree that there has, indeed, been a change of shape. The butterfly lays its eggs in a place that will provide food for them when they hatch. Out of an egg comes a tiny caterpillar, or larva, whose main interest is eating. After several molts, the caterpillar assumes a new guise. It becomes a pupa, sometimes hidden inside a cocoon. During this seemingly lifeless stage, the most amazing changes take place. The tissues of the caterpillar are gradually used up to make the tissues of the adult form.

The words "larva" and "pupa" are Latin words. When there is more than one, we say "larvae" and "pupae."

The advantage of this strange life cycle is that the young can devote all their energy to eating and growing. The adults, because they can fly, can spread over greater areas. They can range farther in search of food, mates, and egg sites. They can escape from some of their enemies. The flying stage of insects is the reproducing and dispersing stage.

Another advantage of metamorphosis is that insects can adapt to the different seasons of the year. Most butterflies, for example, lay their eggs in early summer, and the caterpillars feast on the lush foliage and growing crops. With the coming of autumn, when food is less plentiful, the caterpillar selects a sheltered place and changes into a pupa. The pupa does not need food and lies immobile through the winter. The warm weather and longer days of spring give the signal that it is time for the adults to emerge. The males and females mate, eggs are laid, and the cycle starts again.

Some insects overwinter as eggs, others as larvae or adults. But in every case, the variety of forms during an individual insect's life allows it to tailor its life cycle to the seasons.

The secret of success

We have been discovering some clues to the insects' secret of success. The exoskeleton gives protection, and allows for a variety of structures. The life cycle helps the insect cope with hard times of the year. Winged adults can reach new areas.

So now let us take a look at some of the many different kinds of insects and find out their special secrets. What is their food supply, and how do they escape their enemies? How do they cope with the cold of winter or the heat of summer? What are their young stages like?

Let us enter into the insects' world.

CHAPTER 2

Insects Close Up

WHEN YOU LOOK at the structure of an insect, it seems to be outside in and upside down. We have already seen that the skeleton is on the outside of its body. The heart lies along its back, and its nervous system is along its underside.

You find sense organs in even stranger positions. There are insects that hear with their knees, smell with their feelers, and some even taste with their feet!

The head

Find a fairly large insect, such as a grasshopper, and look at it face to face. Like you, it has eyes and a mouth but it does not have a nose. In the previous chapter, we saw that an insect breathes through tiny holes in its body. It can smell with two hornlike feelers, or *antennae*. These antennae also have a good sense of touch. Watch the way an ant uses them as it explores.

INSECTS CLOSE UP • *19*

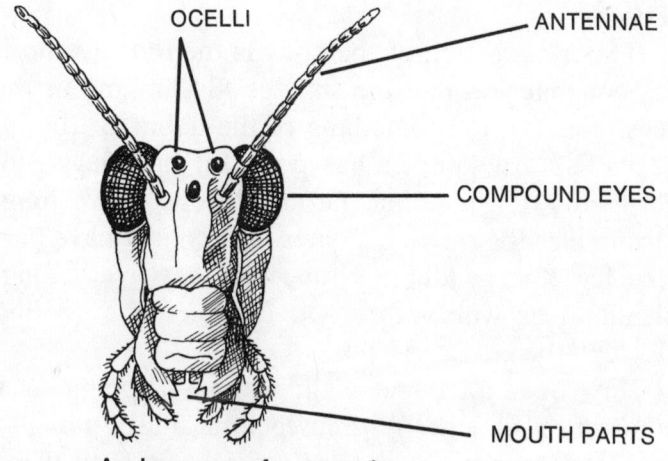

A close-up of a grasshopper's head.

The eyes are often huge. They are made up of many little six-sided lenses and are called *compound* eyes. Through them, the insect gets a mosaic picture of the world. There may also be one to three small eyes, called *ocelli.*

The mouthparts are the most difficult to identify. They vary with the kind of food the insect eats. The basic plan is an upper lip or *labrum,* a lower lip or *labium,* and two pairs of jaws that work sideways, called *mandibles* and *maxillae.* Grasshoppers and beetles have strong chewing jaws. Butterflies have mouthparts suitable for sipping nectar. The maxillae form a long, coiled tongue. Mosquitoes, as you no doubt know, have sharp mouthparts that can pierce your skin and suck your blood. These piercing and sucking parts are protected by a sheath formed by the labium.

Thorax

The next section of the body is the *thorax,* and it is here that you find the six legs. By looking at the legs, you can tell something of the habits of the insect. The grasshopper has powerful hind legs—all the better for jumping. Ground beetles have long, strong legs for running. Water insects may have oar-like legs for paddling. Crane flies have very long, slender legs which are good for finding a footing down in the grass.

How does an insect walk without tripping over some of its six legs? With insects that hurry along— ants and beetles—it is hard to see how they place their feet. If you can get hold of some stick insects,

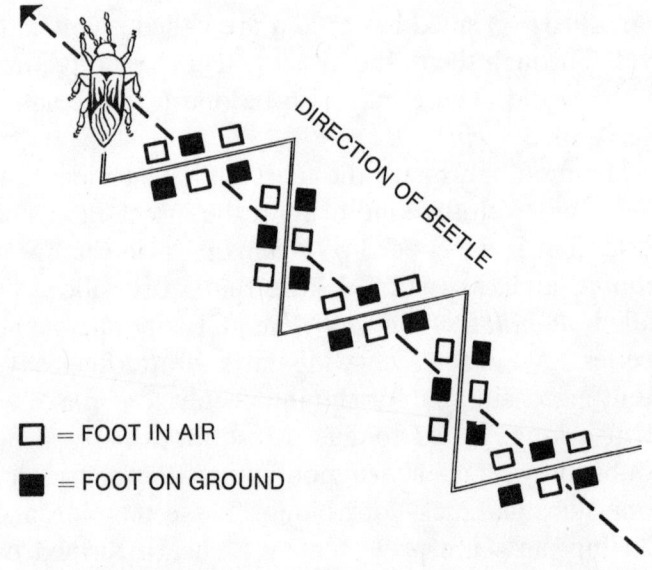

A diagram showing how an insect walks.

you will find that they move fairly slowly, and you can watch the rhythm of their legs. Stick insects shed their legs easily and, in almost any population, there are a few that are missing one or more legs. How do the missing legs affect the order in which they move their feet?

When an insect walks, it actually zigzags with each step. You can see this if you allow a beetle to walk through some food coloring and then across a piece of paper. Catch the beetle in a pitfall trap (*see* Chapter 8) and then chill it in the refrigerator for a little while, to make it easier to handle. Have it walk through a little pool of color, making sure that the tip of the abdomen gets wet. You will see the zigzag trail as it runs across the paper. Does the beetle appear to run on the very tips of its feet, or does it leave longer tracks on the paper?

Wings

The wings are also found on the thorax. In all other animals that fly, the wings are arms or legs that have taken on a new shape, but insects' wings are not modified legs. They are outgrowths of the thorax. The earliest insects must have glided on flaps—probably three pairs. Then the second and third pair developed joints at the body and muscles which allowed the wings to move up and down. Insects no longer glided on fixed wings but could really fly.

In the most primitive insects, the fore and hind wings move separately. You can see this in dragonflies. Butterflies, moths, and wasps have the fore and hind wings locked together so that they work as one pair. Flies only have the one pair—the front wings.

Some insects are very good fliers and cover great distances during their short lives. Monarch butterflies may travel 2000 miles. Even some of the weakest insects can cover great distances. These are tiny creatures such as thrips and aphids that drift in the wind and are sometimes carried right across oceans.

Insects vary, too, in the way they hold their wings when at rest. Again, it is the dragonflies that have the simplest and most primitive way of resting—with the wings lying horizontally. Can you find examples of insects that close their wings straight up over their bodies? Do you know any that lay their wings flat along their backs. Some close their wings so that they form a tent over them. Beetles have developed hard wing covers called *elytra*. The wings they use for flying are the thin, transparent hind wings, and they tuck these under the protective covers. Watch a ladybird alight, and you can often see it tuck the last folds of its wings under the spotted elytra.

It is a fascinating sight to watch an insect expand its wings for the first time when it emerges from its pupal skin. The new adult looks ill-formed and ugly with its large, soft body and small, crumpled wings. Gradually, the muscles force blood into the wings, and they expand and harden. Then the insect is ready for the adventure of flight.

Flying takes a lot of energy. A bumblebee has to "rev" up on a cold morning. You can watch this for yourself if you chill a bumblebee in the refrigerator and then put it outside on a warm day. It does not fly right off, but vibrates its wings. How long does it vibrate?

With a stopwatch you can time a fly buzzing around in a room. How long does it fly between rests? Does it always buzz around for the same length of time? What makes it stop flying? Could it be fatigue or the attraction of food? Does it often choose the same resting place? Does it fly for longer periods in a warm or a cool room?

Catch a fly and glue it to a toothpick so that its legs and wings are free. You can work on a chilled surface to slow the fly down while you do this. Now place the fly so that its feet are on the table. The wings come to rest. When you lift the legs free, you will find that the wings automatically fly.

In spite of the obvious advantages of being able to fly, there are insects in almost every group that have lost the power of flight. Ants have no need for wings in their underground nests. Fleas, living in a forest of hair, would find wings in the way. Some female moths are wingless, but the males can fly. One reason for this may be that these moths emerge early in the season when the weather is often stormy. If they could fly, they might easily be carried away from their food plants before laying their eggs. The males have to take this chance when they fly to look for a mate. The loss of some males is not so harmful to the species as the loss of the egg-bearing females would be.

There are a few insects that never developed wings in the whole course of their history. The silverfish that creeps about the kitchen shelves is one of the most primitive insects you will find. Neither it nor its ancestors were ever able to fly. Silverfish change very little as they grow—a young silverfish is very similar to the adult.

The abdomen

Behind the thorax is the abdomen. It is divided into sections or *segments*. The highest number of segments you will find is 11. At the end of the body is the *anus* where undigested food is passed out. The insect may have tail feelers on its last segment that are sensitive to touch and sound vibrations. Covering the body are hairs or *setae* which allow the insect to sense the world around it.

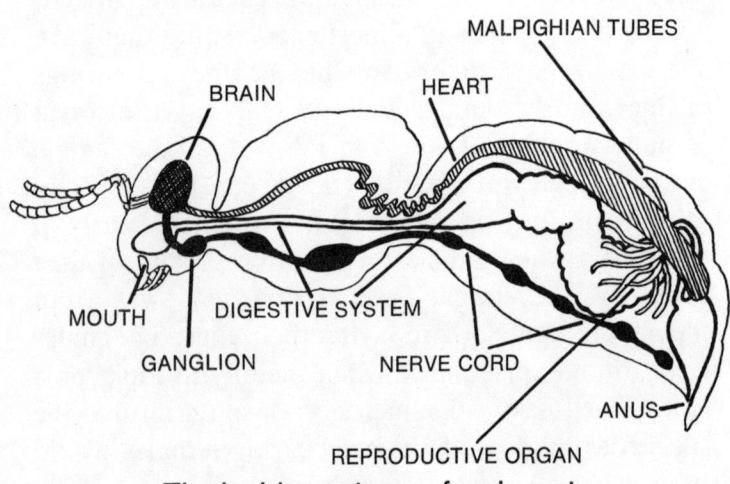

The inside anatomy of an insect.

Inside the abdomen are the digestive system and the sex organs. There are also nerves, fat body, heart, and blood. If you have a big insect such as a large grasshopper or a cockroach, you can open it up and find some of its organs.

You can kill the insect by dropping it into very hot water and then freezing it solid. Cut it in two, lengthwise, with a razor blade, and you will see some of its organs. You might try this with a large caterpillar.

To study the digestive and other systems, you will want to do a dissection. The best way to hold the insect for dissection is to pour melted wax into a tin lid. When the wax has almost set, place the insect, legs down, in the wax. Allow the wax to harden. Remove the wings, and then make a cut along the side, pulling back the skin and pinning it down. A pair of sharp manicure scissors and fine forceps are good tools. If you fill the lid with salt water (2 rounded teaspoons of table salt to a cup of water), then the organs will float free of each other, and you will be able to see them better.

The tracheae, or air tubes, show up as silvery threads. The digestive system is like a tube with swollen and narrow places that runs from the mouth to the anus. There is a *crop,* or stomach, where digestive juices dissolve parts of the food. A group of fine *Malpighian tubes* act rather like our kidneys, filtering wastes out of the blood and passing them into the hind intestine.

You should look for the creamy white nerve cord

which runs down the underside of the body. The brain is in the head, but all along the nerve cord are nerve centers or *ganglia* (one is a *ganglion*). These receive messages from the body hairs. Because ganglia receive and process messages, the brain is not as important as our brains. An insect can live without a brain. A moth without a brain can lay eggs, but it will not lay them on the right food plant. An insect without a brain can eat, but it cannot find its own food.

Our blood is red because it contains hemoglobin, a chemical which carries oxygen around our bodies. Insects' blood is yellow, or green, or colorless because, with their system of tracheae for breathing, they do not need hemoglobin to carry oxygen. The blood carries food to all parts of the body and takes away wastes. A long, tubular heart along its back draws the blood from the body cavity and pulses it forward to the head.

Do not be discouraged if you cannot find all these organs in your dissection. It is important to know what goes on inside, but you can really learn more by watching live insects. Studying how they react to flowers and lights and sounds tells you about their senses, too.

CHAPTER 3

Insects on the Night Shift

A GOOD WAY to meet a variety of insects is to wait until after dark. When the sun goes down, and the bees have returned to their hive, and the butterfly has found a safe roost for the night, then you can meet the night shift. Moths flutter at the window and crickets chirp in the grass.

You do not need to grope in the dark to find these evening insects. They are mostly attracted to lights, and you find them circling the porch light or crawling on a lighted window. Scientists say they are *positively phototactic*—they move toward the light.

Moths find their way by the light of the stars. They fly so that the light rays always strike their eyes at the same angle. The stars are so far away that the light rays reaching the earth from them are almost parallel to each other. Moths developed this type of navigation long before man invented his confusing artificial lights. When a moth tries to steer by a light that is close—such as a street light—the rays from it

28 • EXPLORING THE INSECT WORLD

are not parallel. The moth has to turn to keep the rays striking its eyes at the same angle, and it spirals into the light (*see* diagram).

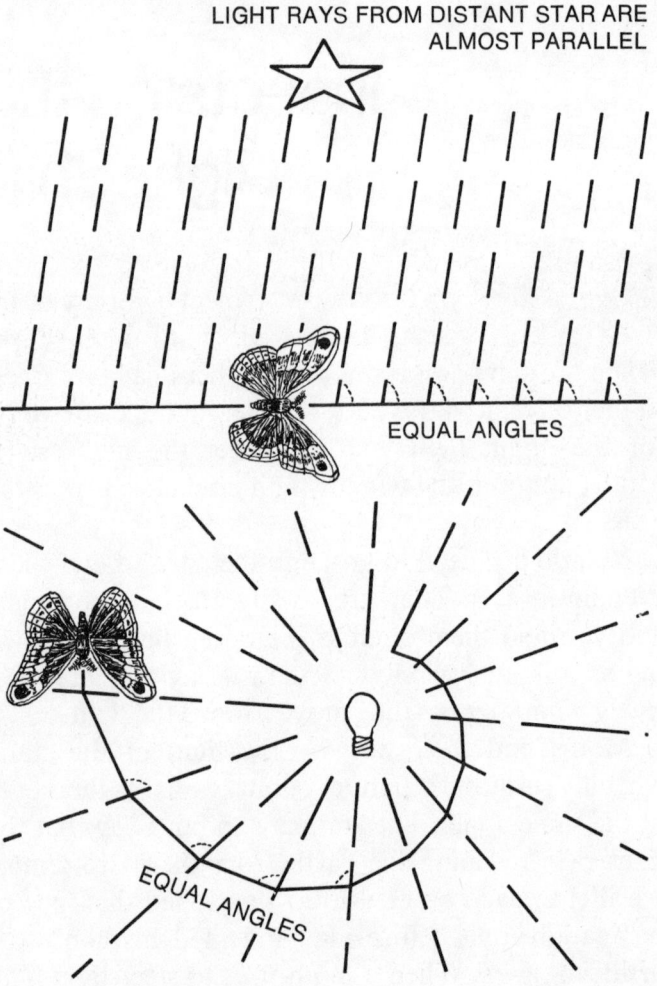

How a moth spirals around a streetlamp.

A light trap

You can attract moths and other insects by using this "spiraling" effect of light on their flight. A simple light trap can be made with an electrical extension cord, a lamp, and a piece of white sheet. Hang the sheet behind the lamp. Some of the insects circling around will settle on the sheet, and you will get a chance to look at them. Are you getting mostly moths, or beetles, or little midges?

A light trap for collecting insects.

Make a count of the insects that settle on the sheet in, say, 15 minutes. Try it again the next night. Some nights are buzzing with activity, while others are quiet. Can you find a reason for this? The thermometer might give you a clue. Or is there a breeze?

Is there bright moonlight? Do a little detective work and find out how the weather affects the activity of night insects.

You can also use a light trap to find out if the same kinds of insect fly at night from spring to fall. Does the June "bug" fly only in June, or can you catch it in August?

To answer such questions, you can make a more elaborate light trap with which you can actually catch the insects (so that you can identify them). Then you do not have to stay and watch for them. Entomologists often use a trap such as the one in the diagram. In the middle is a fluorescent tube with four "baffles" set at right angles to each other. The insects circling the light hit the baffles and then drop into the collecting can, which contains poison.

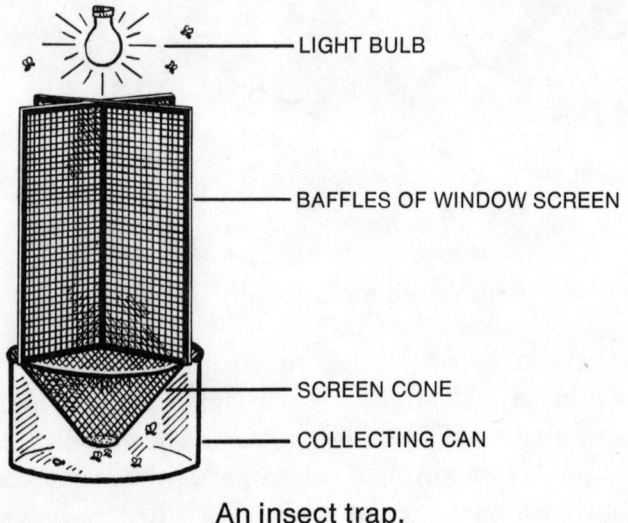

An insect trap.

You can make a simpler trap with baffles set below an ordinary light bulb. A can with a little water and detergent makes a trap under the baffles. If you want to trap the insects alive put a cone of wire or window screening in the can. The stunned insects will drop down and not be able to find their way out.

Colored lights

Scientists have found that insects are more attracted to some colors of light than to others. In fact, insects almost ignore some colors. This interests entomologists. They want to know what color of light will *attract* most insects. It interests almost everyone else because they want to know what color of light will keep insects *away*.

You could try to find out what color of light attracts most insects. You might simply try replacing your porch light with different-colored bulbs and counting the insects that come circling around. There is a problem with this method, however. If you have used the light trap, you will have found that some nights are good for collecting insects, and some are poor. If you try a yellow light on a night that hums with action, and a green one the following evening when few insects are active, can you then say that yellow is better than green for attracting insects?

One way to get around this problem is to check the weather, temperature, and the brightness of the moon and test the different colors of light on nights when these are about the same. The best way,

32 • EXPLORING THE INSECT WORLD

A Christmas light experiment using different colored lights for attracting insects.

though, is to compare the effects of the colored lights on the *same* night. You can try to do this by hanging up a string of outdoor Christmas tree lights. Use four bulbs—red, yellow, green, blue—separated as far as possible along the cord. Attach a paper plate behind each bulb, using tape to hold it in place. Lay strips of sticky "flypaper" across each plate so that insects landing on them will be caught. Then switch the lights on and wait. After an hour or so, count the catch on each plate.

Test the effects of the bulbs on several nights; and remember, the insects may be attracted by a bulb's brightness as well as by its color. Once you have discovered which bulb attracts the greatest number of insects, you can use that color of bulb in your light trap.

Fireflies

While you are out looking at your light trap, you may find an insect that is using the same idea. It is the firefly. It has a built-in light to attract its mate.

The firefly is really a type of beetle. The larva feeds on snails and slugs. It paralyzes them before beginning its meal. In many species, the adult female looks just like the larva, and is called a "glowworm." Only the male develops wings and flies off in search of a mate. The female, down in the grass, can use her light to signal to the male above. He gives an answering signal—the dancing light you see flickering in the evening.

If you watch carefully, you will find there is a pattern in the flash signal of the firefly, and each species has its own code of flashes. In fact, many species of firefly look so much alike that you can only tell them apart by their flash signal. The female sometimes uses this in a surprising way. Down in the grass, she gives the mating signal of *another* species of firefly. A male answers. She signals again, and the male comes nearer. When she has lured him to the ground, she eats the poor, unsuspecting male for supper!

Once you have learned the firefly code you, too, might be able to fool a male firefly. Notice not only the flashes but the length of time between the flashes. Cover a flashlight bulb so that there is only a small point of light, and then flash out the code.

How bright is a firefly light? In some countries, natives use "firefly torches" to light their way through the jungle. You could try putting a firefly or glowworm on a printed page and see how many letters it lights up with its flash. Does it flash with the same pattern and brightness when it is disturbed?

Does oxygen affect its brightness? You could test this by letting a small candle burn under a glass jar. The flame will die out when the oxygen is used up. When the jar is cool, tilt it enough to slip in a few fireflies. Compare the light of these beetles with the same number in a jar where no candle has burned.

Does temperature affect the brightness of its light? Try laying a firefly on an ice cube. What happens to the light?

The light from an electric bulb or a flame makes heat as well as light. But the light of a firefly is *cold* light. The substances that make the firefly light are called *luciferin* and *luciferase*.

Sugaring

Some flowers stay open at night and are visited by moths. You will notice that most of these evening-blooming flowers are white or pale yellow—colors that show up well in the moonlight. And many of them are scented. Night insects are attracted by smells as well as by light.

This gives a clue to another way to collect insects at night. For this, you need some overripe fruit—peaches or bananas are best. Mash them with a tablespoon of brown sugar. After a few hours, this mixture will be just right for attracting insects. Toward evening, "paint" the mixture on a post or tree trunk, and then wait for darkness. Entomologists call this way of collecting insects *sugaring*. After dark, go back to the bait with a flashlight and see what you can find. Moths, ants, beetles—perhaps, a cockroach? The cockroach will scuttle away from your flashlight, for it is *negatively phototactic*. It is repelled by light.

Attracting male moths

Some night insects rely on their sense of smell for finding food. Others find their mates, using their sense of smell. The most dramatic example of this is found among some of the moths. The male can smell the scent of a female 3 miles away, yet you cannot smell her in the same room!

Some moths that find their mates this way are the Luna, the Oak Eggar, the Emperor, and certain hawk moths. The males have very feathery antennae and use them for smelling. The females have scent organs near the tip of the body.

If you put a newly emerged female in a wire cage and put it outside on a warm evening, you will find male moths swarming round the cage. One experimenter marked male moths and then released them up to 2 miles away from the caged female. By the time he got home, the male moths were already there.

Scientists call this ability "assembling," and there is still much to be discovered about it. They do not know all the species that do it, nor how the weather affects their ability to smell. If you try putting out unmated female moths, remember that they must be in cages that allow their scent to travel. A moth in a jar will not attract any suitors. Also, there is only a short period in each 24 hours when the males are on the wing.

The insect chorus

When you are out hunting insects at night, you will hear the sounds of insects, too. See if you can find the insects that are making the sounds you hear. The male field cricket makes music with his wings, and the female listens with ears on her knees.

If you can get to know the song of the snowy tree cricket, then you can tell the temperature by using a watch with a second hand. Count the number of chirps the cricket makes in 15 seconds, add 40, and you have the temperature in degrees Fahrenheit. Check the temperature with a thermometer and see how accurate the cricket is.

You may hear the hum of a mosquito. That is the female mosquito calling a mate. She makes the sound by the rapid beat of her wings. She needs a meal of blood before she lays her eggs. So you do not need a light trap or overripe peaches to attract the mosquito. You are the bait!

CHAPTER 4

Plants and the Insects They Need

YOU WERE ABLE to find insects at night by attracting them to a light. During the day, you can find even more insects—if you know where to look. A good place to start is a small flowering shrub. See how many different kinds of insects you can find on it. If you search the flowers, buds, leaves, and stems, you may count as many as a dozen kinds.

Do all these insects live there "rent free"? The plant is probably providing them with protection, food, and a place to lay their eggs. Do the insects do anything for the plant?

The fact is that there would not be nearly so many kinds of plants if it were not for insects.

During the millions of years that plants and insects have been on earth, amazing partnerships have formed. Members of the two groups have, in many cases, become completely dependent on one another. When you look at the chewed leaf of a cabbage or find a worm in an apple, you can easily see how the plant benefits the insect. But what is it that makes insects important to plants?

Plants evolved their showy, sweet-smelling flowers long before man was on earth to enjoy them. Flowers, with their lovely patterns of shapes and colors and smells, were developed for one reason—to attract insects. They need insects.

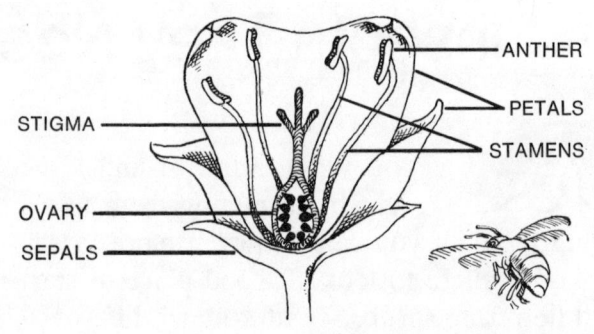

Parts of a flower.

If you look carefully at a flower, you will find there is more to see than just bright petals. Pull off the petals and look for the *stamens*. The top part of the stamen is the *anther,* and this contains *pollen.* Now pull off the stamens, and you will be left with the *pistil*. It is usually vase-shaped. The top is called the *stigma,* and the lower, swollen, part is the *ovary* where the seeds will develop.

The role of the insect is to transfer the pollen from the anthers of one plant to the stigmas of another. This is called *pollination,* and, without it, the seeds would not form in the ovary. New plants could not grow.

Bees at work

You can learn quite a lot about pollination simply by watching the insects in a flower garden. The pollinators fall into four different insect orders. The most important flower pollinators are the bees, and they, along with wasps and ants, belong to the order *Hymenoptera* (membrane wings).

Bees eat only two things—nectar and pollen. Both of these they get from flowers. Honeybees, as you probably know, live and work together as a colony. The bees you see flying around flowers are the workers, and their job is to take honey back to the hive where it is used for food. The extra is stored for wintertime when no flowers bloom.

Take a look at a honeybee—but do this cautiously because bees sting. One way to catch one is to put a drop of honey inside a jar lid and set the lid near where bees are flying. When a bee lands on the lid, use the jar to trap it.

You will notice that a bee is quite a hairy creature. Pollen clings easily to its furry body and legs so the bee does its job of pollination well. Look for the "pollen baskets" on the hind legs. These are wide, flat places where the bee can pack the pollen to carry it back to the hive. There, other workers mix the pollen with honey and feed it to the larvae. You may be able to see the pollen on the legs of bees flying around flowers. You will see that the color can vary from orange to white. Do all the bees visiting the same flowers have the same color of pollen in their baskets?

If your captive bee tastes the honey, you will see that it has an unusual tongue. It is long, rather like a drinking straw, and ends in a little, hairy "spoon." The bee can extend its tongue to reach the nectar in different types of flowers.

Let your bee go and see what you can find out by watching bees as they fly around the flowers. Make a note of the different kinds of flowers visited by bees. Do they have a perfume? What does this tell you about a bee's sense of smell? What colors of flowers do bees visit? Keep a record for several weeks and see if you can learn which colors attract bees. Chapter 9 tells you more about bees and colors.

Follow the flight of a single bee as it goes from one flower to another. Does it keep to the same kind of flower?

Flies and beetles

Sometimes, when you are looking for bees, you might be fooled by a fly. The hover fly has the same coloring as a bee and is also a nectar feeder. It has, however, only one pair of wings. It belongs to the same order as house flies—*Diptera* (two wings). You can tell hover flies from bees and wasps by the size and shape of their antennae (*see* diagram).

You often see hover flies visiting blue flowers. You can test if it is the color of the flower that attracts them by placing pieces of blue paper and pieces of gray close to the flowers. Do they ever mistake the blue paper for the flowers? Do they ever visit the gray papers?

PLANTS AND THE INSECTS THEY NEED • *41*

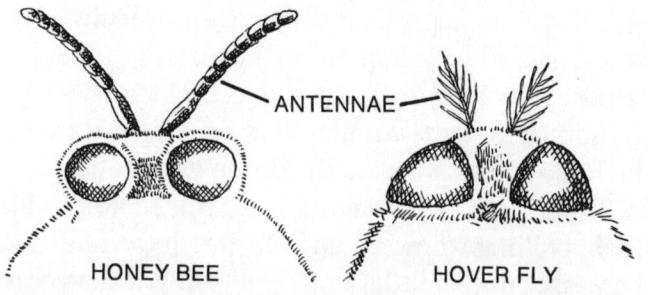

HONEY BEE — ANTENNAE — HOVER FLY

Bees have different antennae than houseflies.

The most interesting thing about hover flies is the way they can stay poised in midair over a flower. Their wings vibrate too fast to see, and they dart from place to place so suddenly that they seem to vanish.

You can make a cage for a hover fly and watch its flight. Use a glass gallon jar of the type that comes with vinegar or apple juice. Wash it and then make sure it is dry. Put strips of masking tape around it as shown in the photograph. This lets the fly get its bear-

Jar for hover fly.

ings inside the jar. When you put a hover fly in this glass cage, it will sometimes hover for quite long periods. How long does it stay in one place?

Another fly that you may find on the flowers, and which looks like a bee, is the drone fly. It often visits the flowers of Queen Anne's lace. But there are flies which pollinate flowers and do not look like bees. These are mostly little gnats and midges that crawl into the flowers and become coated with pollen.

There is an orchid that is specially designed to trap little flies. The petals are so smooth that the small flies slide down into the flower where they brush against the anthers. A tiny back door lets them out and they carry the pollen to other flowers.

Do you think that fly-pollinated flowers use perfume as a way of attracting flies? Remember that what may smell good to a fly may not smell good to you!

Beetles are members of another insect order, called *Coleoptera*. You can recognize them by their hard wing cases. Some beetles pollinate flowers. They have short tongues, so you find them on flowers where the nectar is easy to reach—like Queen Anne's lace and water lilies. Again, give the flowers the "smell test" and see if you can find out what attracts the beetles.

Butterflies and moths

The fourth order of insects that plants depend on is *Lepidoptera*. These are the moths and butterflies, and they are important nectar feeders. Butterflies are able to detect sweetness even in very small quantities. They can tell sugar water from plain water although there is only a tiny amount of sugar in the water. Put out a saucer of water and one of sugar water, and see if you have any butterfly visitors.

A butterfly tastes with its feet. You can do an experiment to show this. If you touch a butterfly's front feet with a brush that has been dipped in a water and sugar solution, it will uncoil its long tongue. Usually, it does not react to being touched with plain water unless it is very thirsty.

The peacock butterfly is a good one to show this, but you can try it with any butterfly you catch. Hold the butterfly's wings between two ½-inch-wide strips of stiff paper as shown in the photograph. A paper clip close to the wings keeps them secure.

The butterfly tasting experiment, showing how the butterfly is held.

The butterfly responds to the sugar water the first two or three times and then seems to get tired. How long does it need to rest before it will respond again?

Make a list of the colors of flowers that are visited by butterflies. Which are the most common colors on your list? Do you think that butterflies have the same range of color vision as bees?

While watching insects on flowers, you have probably seen more butterflies than moths, but this is not because there are more butterflies. In Chapter 3, you found that moths are night fliers.

One of the most interesting pollination stories centers round a small, white moth called *Pronuba*. The larvae of this moth feed on the seeds of the yucca lily. And the tall lily with its spike of fragrant flowers depends on the little moth for pollination. The moth and the lily have a strange partnership.

This is what happens. The female pronuba flies to a blossom, gathers a ball of pollen from the stamens, and flutters off to another flower. There the moth lays four or five eggs among the ovules in the ovary, then climbs onto the pistil and pushes the pollen ball onto the stigma. Other insects pollinate flowers more or less by chance as they search for food, but the pronuba seems to be quite deliberate as she fertilizes the ovules which will grow into seeds. Some of these seeds will provide food for her eggs when they hatch.

Eventually, the caterpillars crawl out of the seed pods and spin cocoons in the soil. Enough seeds are left to grow into new plants. The next year, when the yucca blooms, male and female moths will emerge from the cocoons, mate, and repeat the cycle. It would almost seem that these two partners depend on each other too much. But, each year, the flowers open, and the moths are waiting. Each year, the caterpillars eat some seeds, but only their share.

Investigating pollination

Some plants do not need insects for pollination. For example, corn, grasses, and evergreen trees rely on the wind to blow the pollen from the anther to the stigma. These plants produce great quantities of pollen to make sure that some of it reaches a stigma. If these plants had evolved a different way of pollination, perhaps some of us would be spared hay fever!

Can an insect-pollinated plant get along without insects? You can investigate this question yourself in the spring with a muslin bag or a nylon stocking.

Flowering trees are good for investigating purposes because they set seed fairly quickly and you can see the results. Cherry, apple, or maple all produce lots of flowers on one branch. Tie a bag or a stocking carefully over the branch when the buds begin to swell, but before the flowers open.

Apple and cherry blossoms have the bright petals which are typical of insect-pollinated flowers. What about the small flowers of the maple tree? Can they depend on wind? Tie a stocking over a branch. This will keep insects out but will allow pollen-bearing winds to reach the flowers. In a week or so, the little airplane seeds are developing all over the tree. Take the stocking off and see if there are any seeds on the covered branch.

When apple and cherry trees are in bloom, bees

hover over the blossoms, so you can guess that they are the chief pollinators. Can other insects do the job for them? Tie a few stockings over branches. Remember to do this before the blossoms open. When the tree is in bloom, carefully allow one or two ants into a stocking and then tie it tight again to keep out other insects. You might try ladybirds, or flies, or the little flower beetles on other branches. After the petals have fallen and the bees no longer visit the tree, you can take the stockings off, but tag the branches so that you will know them later. When the small fruits show on the other branches, check your experiments. Did the ants, and beetles, and other insects do the job?

The insect eaters

Some plants need insects in a very different way. They eat them. These plants live in soils that are lacking some of the chemicals that plants need for growth. The plants obtain these chemicals by catching insects and digesting them.

The sundew has a rosette of leaves covered with sticky tentacles. They glitter like dewdrops in the sunshine and give off a slight perfume. An unwary insect lands on the leaf and finds the dewdrops are a sticky trap. It struggles to get free, but this causes the tentacles to give off more of the sticky sap and wrap around the insect, trapping it. Four or 5 days later, the leaf spreads open again, and only the empty skeleton of the insect remains.

Another insect eater is the Venus's-flytrap. Its

PLANTS AND THE INSECTS THEY NEED • *47*

leaves are hinged along the midrib and can snap shut when an insect lands on them. Special hairs on the leaf trigger the trap, and once the insect is caught, its struggles cause glands in the leaf to pour out digestive juices.

Pitcher plants are also insect eaters, but they do not trap the insects. They just lure them by perfume and nectar into their pitcher-shaped leaves. The hairs

A pitcher plant.

at the mouth of the pitcher all point downward, and inside is a pool of liquid. The insect slips down and drowns in the liquid. Digestive juices act on the body of the insect leaving only the skeleton. If you examine the liquid in a pitcher plant, you may find live insects among the skeletons. These would be the larvae of a species of mosquito or midge or fly. These insects have adapted to this very restricted environment and are able to eat and live in this place which is a death trap for most kinds of insects.

You can keep insect-eating plants in a terrarium and find out more about them. They need acid soil and lots of moisture. Some growers or biological supply dealers sell insect-eating plants and give instructions how to care for them.

Keep a record of how they grow and how often they catch insects. Can you fool a sundew with a tiny stone? Can you find the trigger hairs on a Venus's-flytrap? How deep is the water in a pitcher plant? Can an insect ever escape?

CHAPTER 5

The Hungry Horde

WHEN YOU COUNTED the insects on a flowering shrub you found a number of different kinds. Some of these are helpful to the plant. They pollinate the flowers. But others are freeloaders, feasting on the plant tissues without doing anything in return.

We see petals nibbled by beetles, leaves tunneled by leaf miners and chewed by caterpillars, and sap sucked by little, green aphids. It all seems rather unfair to the plant, does it not? But remember that the main job of the plant is to provide for the next generation of plants like itself by producing seeds. As long as the plant is strong enough to produce seeds, it does not matter that it is providing free room and board for these insect guests.

But *we* mind if our prize roses are nibbled, and our cabbages are ragged, and our apples wormy! So we judge the "good" and the "bad" insects by how they affect our lives and not the life of the plant.

Insects may do more than just nibble here and

there. Creeping and crawling and flying armies can strip fields bare, leaving complete desolation. Some of these outbreaks of plant-eating insects are our fault because we grow only one kind of plant over great areas. We have provided a gold mine of food, which causes a rapid increase in the numbers of insects that feed on it. Also, plant breeders look for the biggest and most succulent varieties of plants. Very often, these appeal to the insects as much as they appeal to us.

Even before man farmed crops, there were times when the hungry horde devoured the plants, and few seeds formed to produce the next generation. This is part of nature's strategy. The growth of a species of plant or animal is not a steady thing but part of a cycle that depends on many other plant and animal species.

Let us take a closer look at some of these hungry insects and find out what and how much they eat.

Keeping caterpillars

Among the easiest plant eaters to get to know are the caterpillars of various kinds of moths and butterflies. You can keep these in cages and watch the amazing life story of an insect unfold.

The simplest cage is a quart canning jar. Instead of the inner metal lid, use a piece of cheesecloth held in place by the screw ring. The cloth allows air into the jar. A better rearing cage can be made by filling a flowerpot or a coffee can with garden soil. Take a piece of window screening, bend it into a

A coffee-can rearing cage for caterpillars.

cylinder, and push it into the soil. Use a piece of glass for a top.

When you collect a caterpillar for your cage, notice the kind of plant you find it on, because this will probably be what your caterpillar eats. Many caterpillars will starve rather than feed on another kind of plant. Others will accept a wide range of food.

The caterpillar of the monarch butterfly eats only one kind of leaves. The adult lays its eggs on a milkweed plant. Out of each egg comes a little, striped caterpillar, which immediately begins to eat milkweed leaves. It eats and grows and molts.

Look for monarch caterpillars on a milkweed plant, and take one or two home to your cage. You will notice chewed leaves where the caterpillar has been feeding. Just how much do you suppose a caterpillar eats?

Here is a way to find out.

You will need a sheet of graph paper. The kind divided into ⅒ inches would be best. Before you feed your caterpillar, carefully draw a line round each leaf on the graph paper. The next day, when you change the leaves, lay the ragged, half-eaten leaves back on the pattern you drew the day before. By counting the squares on the graph paper, you can estimate the area of leaves the caterpillar ate (dividing the number of little squares it ate by 100 gives you the number of square inches).

Using this method, you can work out how much food it takes to make a butterfly.

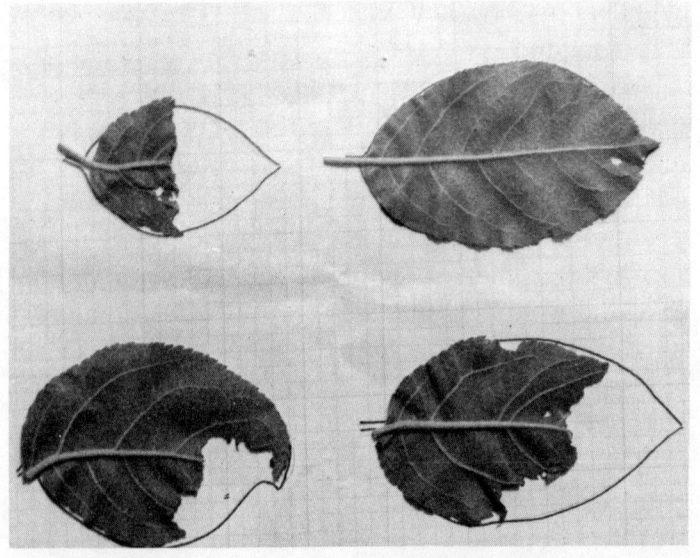

Leaves showing how much caterpillars have eaten.

Some caterpillars will eat different types of leaves. You can compare how much food two caterpillars of the same kind eat on different diets. The cabbage white caterpillar lives, as you might guess, on cabbages. It will also eat nasturtium leaves. Do caterpillars eat the same amount of these different foods? If one eats less, does it then take longer to grow?

Do caterpillars eat more when it is cold or when it is warm? Compare the amount eaten by caterpillars, which are about the same size, kept at different temperatures. By measuring the amount they eat, you can find out whether caterpillars eat mostly during the day or during the night. If there is a difference, could it be due to the nighttime being cooler? You could keep two caterpillars in different jars and put a paper sack over one to find out the effect of darkness when the caterpillars are at the same temperature.

When you are doing investigations like these, it is a good idea to try each one more than once. Just before a caterpillar molts, it does not eat. You can see how this could throw off your results.

After several molts, the caterpillar stops eating and becomes a pupa. You should have a stick in the cage to which the pupa can attach itself. It is a lifeless-looking shell that neither eats nor moves about but, inside that shell, the most wonderful changes are taking place. One day, the pupal case splits open and out crawls a butterfly with a swollen body and crumpled wings. Blood is pumped from the body into the wings, and these gradually harden. The insect has earned its freedom.

Collecting grasshoppers

Another plant eater that you already know is the grasshopper. You can probably catch grasshoppers in your bare hands but using a sweep net makes it easy. Hold the net in front of you and sweep the grass to the right and left as you walk. If you are grasshopper-hunting early in the summer, the grasshoppers in your net will be young ones—but you will recognize them because grasshoppers do not go through the dramatic changes that butterflies do.

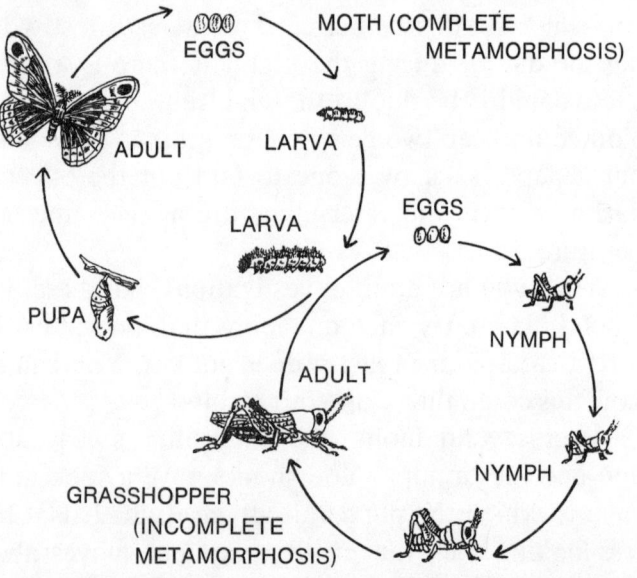

Grasshoppers and moths have different life cycles.

Grasshopper eggs are laid in the earth and hatch with the coming of warm spring weather. The young grasshopper struggles out of the egg case and up through the soil, and is ready for a life of jumping and eating. It is tiny and wingless, and its head looks too big, but it is unmistakably a grasshopper. This young grasshopper is called a *nymph*.

Like caterpillars, the nymphs grow and molt, and, with each molt, there are small changes. By the third or fourth molt, the wings begin to develop; from the final molt, there emerges a grasshopper with full-grown wings.

You can keep a few nymphs in a cage such as the one described for caterpillars and watch these changes with each molt. Food is no problem with grasshoppers because they eat a wide variety. You can give them fresh grass, clover, lettuce, and celery with the leaves left on. See if you can find a way to keep the plants in water without drowning the nymphs. One way to do this would be to use a small bottle for water and push a cotton plug around the stems of the plants.

Try offering the nymphs slices of apple or potato, but remove the food before it gets moldy. Watch the grasshoppers as they eat. Can you see their jaws move? How are their jaws different from ours?

You can measure the length of the nymph at each molt with a set of dividers and a millimeter ruler. Do the grasshoppers molt at the same length on different foods? How much do they grow at a molt? It is easier to measure the cast skin than the newly molted insect.

One of the most noticeable features of the grasshopper is its huge hind legs. They give it its jumping power. Does a frightened grasshopper keep jumping away from danger in a straight line or does it zigzag? How far can a grasshopper jump in relation to its length? How far could *you* jump if you were as good at jumping as a grasshopper?

Grasshoppers can make a noise in two ways. They can make sharp, crackling sounds by rubbing their wings together, either during flight or at rest. Some make a scraping sound by rubbing the inside of the *femur* (the long joint) of the back leg against the edge of the wings. Look at the inner surface of the hind femur. Do you see a ridge of teeth? If you do, the insect probably makes the scraping sounds.

The root feeders

In addition to the insects living on the leaves, flowers, and fruits, there are insects that live under the ground and feed on plant roots. They are mostly the larvae of beetles and flies. They are usually wormlike creatures, streamlined for travel through the soil. One of the most destructive of these is the wireworm—a shiny, yellowish creature. Try digging at the edge of a lawn or examining the roots of weeds and see if you can find any root eaters.

When you are looking in the grass you may find a rather slender, dull-colored beetle. This is the click beetle and is the adult of the wireworm. As if to make up for its destructive youth, the click beetle is an amusing insect. When disturbed, it falls to the ground and "plays possum," lying on its back as if it were dead. Then suddenly, with a click and a jerk, it shoots several inches into the air. It may land on its feet and run away, or it may fall on its back and have to "click" again.

If you look at the underside of a click beetle, you will see a backward-pointing spine on the thorax, which catches against the edge of a cavity. Some kinds of click beetles are much better jumpers than others, so be on the lookout for a champion.

Other plant eaters

A number of insects have sucking mouthparts to pierce the stem or leaves of a plant, and live on the sap. The little green aphids do this. So does the spittle bug. Not only does the spittle bug dine on the sap, but it takes enough extra to provide itself with an air-conditioned room. By blowing air into the sap, it makes a frothy coating, like spit, to protect itself from enemies and the weather. Take a spittle bug out of its froth and put it on another grass stem. How long does it take to make a new "house"?

You may come across leaves marked with blotches and winding lines. This is caused by a leaf miner which actually spends all its young life between the upper and lower surface of a leaf. If you can find a leaf containing a pupa, usually inside a small blister, put the leaf in a jar and wait for the adult to emerge. It will probably be a moth or a fly, and it will, of course, be tiny.

Some insects protect themselves by looking like the plant they live on. There are insects that look like thorns, and leaves, and twigs. There are moths that just seem to disappear when they alight on the bark of a tree.

There are insects such as termites whose appetite for wood has earned them a terrifying reputation. They eat fallen trees and speed up the decay of rotting tree trunks in the forest. Nobody minds that. But when they tunnel into the timber supports and beams in our houses and buildings and turn them to dust, we mind!

So take a careful look at the insects living in the plants around you. Many of them are quite easy to rear and, by doing that, you can learn a lot about them.

CHAPTER

6

Galls—Homes Made to Order

PERHAPS THE STRANGEST of all plant homes are plant galls. They may look like flowers, or cones, or apples, or even little dunce caps. In each case, they are grown by the plant as a home for the larval insect to live in. They do not do the plant any good, but they do provide the insect with a safe shelter and plenty of food.

Different kinds of galls are grown for different kinds of insects. It is often easier to identify the insect by examining its gall than by looking at the insect itself.

Among the commonest galls are the "oak apples" you find on oak trees. These are attached to the leaves or twigs and look like little mottled apples. If you open a young oak apple, you will find the larva of a very tiny wasp. The mother of this wasp larva laid an egg on the growing oak leaves and, at the same time, introduced some chemical substance that caused the gall to start forming. We do not know what these chemicals are, but they change the pat-

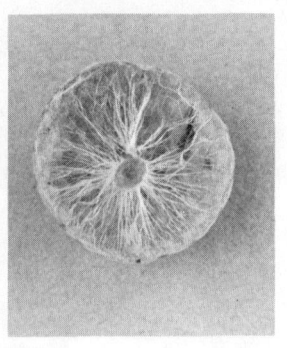

Left: an oak apple.
Right: a cross section of an oak apple.

tern of growth in the plant so that, instead of leaf or stem tissue, the plant grows a fruitlike body rich in food material. If we could learn the secrets of these chemicals, then perhaps, we could grow a new kind of food on oak trees.

For some unknown reason, there are far more kinds of galls found on oak trees than on other

A mossy rose gall.

GALLS—HOMES MADE TO ORDER • *61*

plants. There are also a lot on willows and poplars. Roses and blackberries have a good share, too. This means that a wooded area is a good place to start looking for galls.

You may be able to puzzle your friends by showing them pine cones growing on willow trees. These are galls caused by a small midge, and they do look exactly like cones. The mossy rose gall is a rather pretty gall that you may find on the wild rose or blackberry. It looks like a tuft of reddish moss and is sometimes called "robin's pincushion."

Many of the galls show up best in the winter when the leaves are gone. You may see large, irregular, woody growths which are caused by a fungus, or you may see clusters of twigs called "witches'-broom." These look like old, untidy nests high in the tree and are usually caused by mites. It is not only insects that cause galls.

When you are looking for galls, look at the weeds, too. Goldenrod is a particular favorite of the gall makers. You will find spherical or spindle-shaped

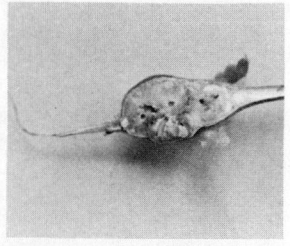

Left: a mint gall.
Right: a cross section of a mint gall.

swellings on several stems in any patch of goldenrod. These, too, show up well on the dead stems in late fall or winter.

A gall collection

You could make a collection of galls. You should identify the plant that the gall came from. You could also try and find out what caused the gall. If there are small holes in it, then the adult insect has emerged. If there are no holes, then keep the gall and see what comes out.

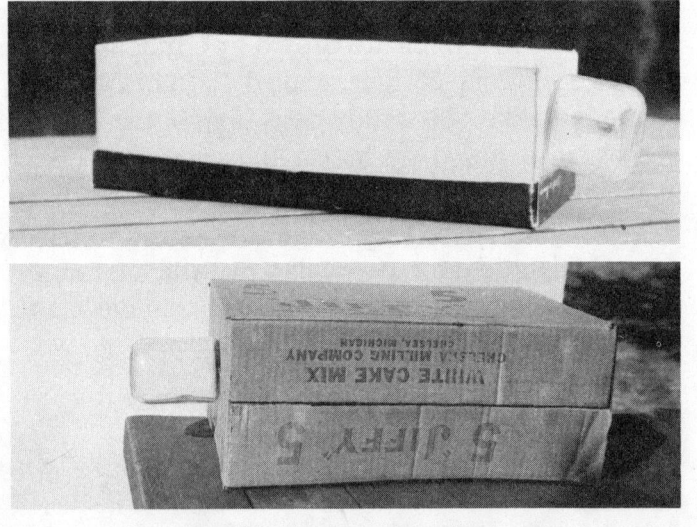

Gall emergence cages.

A good emergence cage can be made from a cardboard box with a hole cut in one side. Insert a jar into the hole. When the adult insects emerge, they are attracted to the light, and you will find them in the jar. You should put a layer of fine soil in the bottom of the box because some insects leave the gall and pupate in the soil. You should moisten the soil occasionally and not leave the container in direct sunlight.

A gall appears to be a very secure home. The walls are thick—often too thick to cut with a pocketknife. Food is rich and plentiful, and the insect never has to leave home to find it. The insects you find in your emergence cage may not be the insects that caused the gall because there are often other insects that want to share this security. Some of these move in as guests and share the food of the host. Others eat the food and the host, too! So you could have several species emerging from the same gall, and then it is a puzzle to know which (if any) started the gall.

Insects that live as guests in other insects' homes are called *inquilines*.

A gall is really a microenvironment—a little environment. The creatures that inhabit it are living in a little world. They are fighting for their share of the food. Some have to die so that others survive.

A study of the life within a gall is a good way to understand ecology. Even in such a very small world, there must be a balance between the living creatures. The insects that emerge from the gall may not be the species that caused the gall, but there must be enough gall makers that survive each year to provide homes for the next generation of inquilines.

Goldenrod galls

If you keep the spindle-shaped goldenrod gall, you will find that a small moth comes out in the fall. The moth mates and then lays its eggs on the old goldenrod stems. In the spring, the eggs hatch, and the tiny caterpillars crawl onto the stems of new plants and burrow into them. A hard, swollen gall grows around the caterpillar. The caterpillar grows and molts within the gall and is soon ready to become a pupa. Before it pupates, it does a strange, but necessary, thing. It cuts a little escape door in the hard gall and covers it with silk. The adult moth has no chewing mouthpart so that the caterpillar must prepare an escape for the adult to avoid being trapped in its own gall.

Jumping galls

One of the most unusual galls is so tiny that most people do not notice it at all. It is attached to the underside of a western oak leaf and is no bigger than a radish seed.

The strange part of the story starts when the gall drops from the leaves early in the summer. It begins to hop and jump about the ground. The larva inside the gall causes it to jump just like a Mexican jumping bean. It jumps about until it lodges in a crack where it will be safe from hungry birds until the adult wasp emerges.

In some places, you will find these galls by the thousands, and they are often called "flea seeds." Different types of jumping galls are found in differ-

GALLS—HOMES MADE TO ORDER • 65

Oak-jumping galls.

ent parts of the United States. They are all very small, but be on the look out for them. They are fun to find.

Pemphigus galls

An interesting gall to study is one caused by the aphid *Pemphigus*. The gall is quite common on poplar trees in late spring. It is a pinkish swelling on the leaf stem, or leaf, about half an inch across. There are several types of *Pemphigus* galls. One is called the "purse gall" and forms halfway up the leaf stem, while another is formed where the leaf and stem meet.

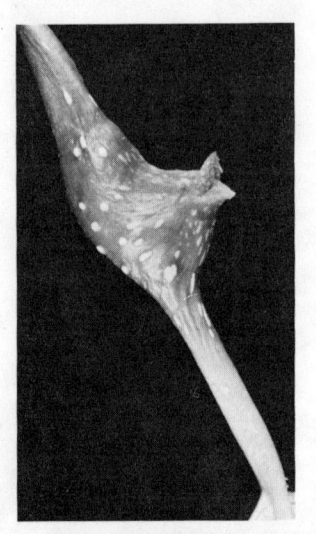

Pemphigus galls. The left is on a lombardy poplar branch, and the right is on a cottonwood. Note extreme curl.

There are usually many of the same kind of gall on one tree. This means that you can break galls open at intervals and find different stages of the gall's story.

Pemphigus gall broken open.

When you open the gall, you will see a small colony of developing aphids. You should be able to spot the "stem mother." She is about five times bigger than the young aphids. It was the stem mother that caused the gall to start growing, and she produced the other aphids. If you break open a different gall every few days, you will find that they are becoming more and more crowded as more young are produced.

Tie small muslin bags over a number of leaves with galls so you can trap the winged aphids when they come out. How many aphids come out of a single gall? Over how many days or weeks do the aphids continue to emerge? Do the biggest galls have the most aphids?

If very few aphids come out of one of the galls, then cut it open and look for an insect that eats aphids. Inside the gall, you will also find the castoff skins of aphids. Each aphid molts five times as it grows, so there will be many skins inside the gall.

There is one insect, called the pirate bug, that eats *Pemphigus* aphids. It goes into the gall and releases a chemical that kills aphids. Then it eats them.

Within the gall, you may find insect guests, or inquilines, which do not harm the aphids but live on the sweet, sticky honeydew that the aphids give off.

When the aphids emerge from the gall, they fly away and find another plant home. The purse gall aphid settles on the roots of lettuce and goes on producing young for the rest of the summer. Then the females return to poplar trees. Each lays one egg which develops into the stem mother the following spring.

Oak apples

The story of the oak apple is even more complicated than the poplar galls. For a long time, it puzzled scientists and, in the case of some galls, their story is still an unsolved mystery.

A tiny wasp lays its eggs on the buds of an oak tree in early spring. A gall starts to form and grows very quickly. Early in the summer, the adult wasps emerge from the gall. These are all females and do not look like the wasp that laid the eggs in the spring. They are, it would seem, breaking a law of nature—animals should grow up to be the same kind of animal as their parents.

These females lay eggs on the leaves, twigs, or

GALLS—HOMES MADE TO ORDER • 69

roots of the oak (according to their species). Galls form, but these are not oak apples. The adults that emerge from these galls are like the first wasps. They mate and lay eggs on the oak buds, and oak apples form again.

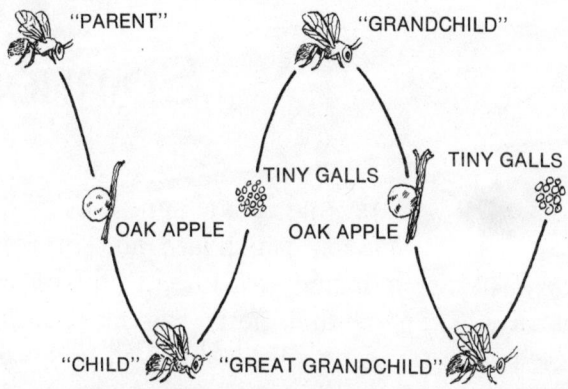

Alternate generations of wasps that make oak galls are alike, but parents and children are not alike.

The diagram will help you understand this complex story. In the life of these wasps, the "parents" and "grandchildren" are alike, causing oak apples in the spring. The children and great-grandchildren are alike, causing small summer galls which last through fall and winter.

You can see that it takes good detective work to follow the life story of the gall wasps. Often, different generations of the same insect have been given different names, and there are still galls where the "missing link" has not been found. The study of galls is difficult, but exciting.

CHAPTER 7

The Silk Spinners

THE GREATEST SPINNERS are the spiders, which are not, of course, insects. They spin a fine silk thread and use it in many ways. They line their nests, trap prey, and protect their eggs by using silk. They even make parachute journeys on a silken thread. We, too, have found a use for spider silk. It is used on gun sights to make the fine cross markings.

There are insect spinners, too. The silkworm is the most famous, and the Chinese have been rearing silkworms for thousands of years. The adult insect is a moth. The silk is formed by the larva when it spins its cocoon and becomes a pupa. The silk unwound from one cocoon can measure 3000 feet. It is spun into thread and then woven into cloth.

There are other moths which spin silk cocoons. One that you might be able to find is the *Cecropia* moth. (The larva may feed on cherry, plum, apple, maple, birch, or willow. The cocoon is attached to a twig close to where the larva was feeding.) If you can find one, keep it till spring and see the great moth emerge.

Quite a number of insects use silk to tie leaves together to form a shelter. One larva makes a tube out of pine needles, binding them with silk. Some insects use naturally curled leaves as a home, while others roll their own homes. The insect spins threads across the leaf, and, as these dry, they shrink and pull the sides of the leaf together. You can watch this if you take a young larva from its rolled leaf and put it on a new leaf.

Often the leaf roller feeds on the leaf tissue of the rolled leaf, leaving a brown skeleton leaf. Other species may reach out of their shelter and feed on nearby leaves.

Usually, the insect forms its pupa within the rolled leaf. When the adult has emerged, the leaf then becomes a home for other insects, such as earwigs. So you never know what you may find within a curled leaf.

Tent caterpillars

The most elaborate homes are made by the tent caterpillars. Instead of each caterpillar making its own home, these caterpillars build a communal shelter where they live in a group. They sleep together in their silk tent and even go out together for meals.

They build their shelters in trees such as chokecherry, birch, alder, apple, and poplar. The tents sometimes measure 2 feet around. Watch for them in the spring. When you find one, you can begin to investigate the lives of the unusual insects that live inside.

The tent caterpillars you find in the spring had their beginnings the summer before, when a female moth laid about 200 eggs around a twig, in a bandlike collar. The eggs were covered with a hard, shiny varnish. This protected them through the winter.

The tiny caterpillars come out of the eggs just as the buds on trees are opening in the spring. For several days, they lead a carefree life, exploring the branch and eating their first meals of tender leaves.

After a few days, they gather together in a mass. Each caterpillar is about ¼-inch long. They settle into a routine that lasts throughout the rest of their caterpillar life. They spin a matlike floor of silk in a crotch of a tree, then roof it over. As the caterpillars grow and need a bigger tent, they use the old roof as their new floor and add another roof and sides.

These tents are easy to see in the spring. When you find one, watch it and keep a record of what you see. Make a note of the activities of the caterpillars at different times of the day.

Dr. R. E. Snodgrass, an entomologist, studied tent caterpillars. He found that the caterpillars lead very organized lives. They started their day early. The caterpillars left for "breakfast" about 6:30 A.M., marching in columns toward the end of the twigs, where they fed for about 2 hours. After breakfast, the caterpillars did a little spinning on the tent. Then they all went inside. Some appeared for "lunch" and did a little more spinning. But the busiest time of the day was just before "dinner," when all the caterpillars gathered on the roof and worked on the tent. Then, as if answering a dinner bell, they all made their way to the feeding grounds.

See if you can find a routine in the eating habits of the caterpillars you watch. There are several species of tent caterpillar, so your findings may not be the same as those of Dr. Snodgrass. Once you know the caterpillars' pattern, you can watch for changes in it and try to find the reason for the changes. For example, do the caterpillars keep to their schedule in wet and cool weather, or do they stay in the tent?

You will have no trouble spotting the feeding grounds, because the caterpillars strip many leaves from the branches. Can you find out how far the caterpillars travel from the tent to food? How much do the caterpillars eat in a day? When the caterpillars travel, they lay down a path of silk and then follow it back to the tent. With your fingers, rub a branch clean at some point between the caterpillars and their tent. Then see how the caterpillars act when they come to the broken trail. Can they find the tent?

The caterpillars molt six times as they grow. During molting, you will notice that the caterpillars stay in the tent for about 2 days.

As the caterpillars get bigger, they need more food. By the time they shed their skins for the last time, they have such an appetite that dinner lasts through the night.

The caterpillars' need for the tent is almost over.

They lose interest in spinning. After about a week, they leave the tent for good. Each caterpillar walks to the end of a twig and steps off, as if it were "walking the plank" in a pirate ship. It drops to the ground on a thread of silk. Then it looks for a hiding place and spins a cocoon. In about 3 weeks, a small brown moth emerges from the cocoon.

As the caterpillars scatter, collect a few and put them in jars with some twigs as supports for the cocoons they will spin. You might try moving some caterpillars to a jar early in their lives. Give them plenty of leaves from the tree on which you found them. Can you raise them away from their colony? Do they try to spin a tent of their own? Do they develop at the same rate as the caterpillars in the tree?

Fall webworm

There is another tent-spinning caterpillar, called the fall webworm. Its tent usually appears later in the year than that of tent caterpillars.

There is an easy way to tell them apart. Fall webworms build their tent over leaves at the ends of branches, and use the leaves in the tent as food. They do not leave the tent to eat. You cannot observe their eating habits, but you can try to raise some on tree leaves.

The adult is a pretty, satiny, white moth, sometimes marked with dark spots.

Follow the leader

About 100 years ago, a French naturalist, Jean

Henri Fabre, thought up a fascinating experiment with silk-spinning caterpillars. Close to his home were some pine trees infested with pine processionary caterpillars, so-called because they march in processions.

Fabre watched them. When they went out to feed, they walked single file, laying down a path of silk as they traveled. The first caterpillar groped along, choosing the way. The other caterpillars followed, in an unquestioning manner, each adding its dribble of silk to the road. Which caterpillar became the leader was just a matter of chance.

Fabre wondered what would happen if there was no leader. If they walked in a closed circle, then every caterpillar would be a follower. But how could he manage to get the caterpillars to walk in a circle?

The answer came by chance. In his greenhouse were some huge palm vases, measuring about 1½ yards around. One day, a procession of caterpillars made its way up the vase and walked around the rim. Fabre waited until the leader completed the circle, with a line of caterpillars following. He knocked off other caterpillars that were still climbing the vase and wiped away any silk connection between the rim and the ground.

He had a complete circle of caterpillars, each following the one ahead, around the rim. The original leader had become an anonymous member of the group. Round and round, round and round they walked, always adding a silken thread to the silken highway.

Fabre wondered how long it would be until one of the caterpillars, driven by hunger, broke the charmed circle. The caterpillars walked all day. Night came and they rested. The morning sun roused them and all that day they walked around the road to nowhere. The next night was cold and the caterpillars huddled in groups. Surely, this would be a chance for the more adventurous to leave the trail and search elsewhere for food. But once again, the column formed and the march continued.

Fabre was astonished at the result of his experiment. He could scarcely believe that the caterpillars could be so stupid. They walked round the rim for 5 days—5 days without food or shelter. They circled the rim 335 times.

The sixth day was mild, following a very cold night. Many of the caterpillars were too weary to walk. The circle broke into small groups, each with a leader. Some of these leaders, at last, plunged over the rim and found the way back to food and shelter.

Usually, it is the caterpillar's ability to follow the silk path that keeps it with the group and leads it to safety. This time, that instinct nearly cost them their lives.

CHAPTER

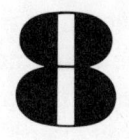

8

The Insect Hunters

HUNTING SEASON lasts all summer long in the grassy jungles. You have been finding insects everywhere—above the ground and under the ground, on leaves and under leaves and inside leaves, on flowers and in flowers. At least, some of these insects you find live by eating other insects. This is just as well because, without them, there would be far, far too many insects.

Insects that feed on other insects are called *predators*. The insects they eat are the *prey*. There are also *parasites*, which grow up at the expense of other insects. The eggs hatch and develop on the tissues of the growing larva, which is called the *host*, though its guests are far from welcome. The parasitic insects are often hard to study because they are so small. When a whole family does all its growing inside a caterpillar, they are not going to grow up to be very big!

So we will start with the predators because they are easier to get to know. A good example is the carabid or ground beetle. It is a large, shiny, black beetle, and it has the characteristics you would expect of a hunter. It can run fast on long legs. It has long antennae, large eyes, and big, powerful jaws.

Ground beetles, as you would guess, do their hunting on the ground and eat soil insects. An easy way to catch them is by setting *pitfall* traps. Sink a jar or a tin can into the ground. The rim of the trap should be level with, or below, the surface of the ground. See that there are no spaces round the outside edge.

A pitfall trap for ground beetles.

You can use the pitfall traps to find out about the habits of ground beetles. Put out traps in several different types of areas—under trees, in a patch of weeds, near a lawn, on bare earth. Check the traps night and morning. Do you think that ground beetles do most of their hunting by night or by day? Which type of area seems to suit the hunter best?

Try keeping a ground beetle in a large jar for a few days and see if you can watch it eat. Put a layer of leaf mold in the bottom of the jar and a piece of wood for the beetle to hide under. Plant a clump of grass or weed and sprinkle this with water so that your beetle can drink. Put some small grubs or caterpillars in the jar as prey. What senses do you think the beetle uses to find the prey? Does it seem to smell it, or hear it, or see it?

You might even be able to get your beetle to eat some raw hamburger. Remember, too, that beetles can fly, so you will need to cover the cage.

The praying mantis

The most awesome of the insect killers is the praying mantis. It has such a frightening appearance that you might think twice about trying to keep one in a cage, but the mantis is quite harmless—to you. To other insects, however, the praying mantis spells sudden death. It will even eat other mantises.

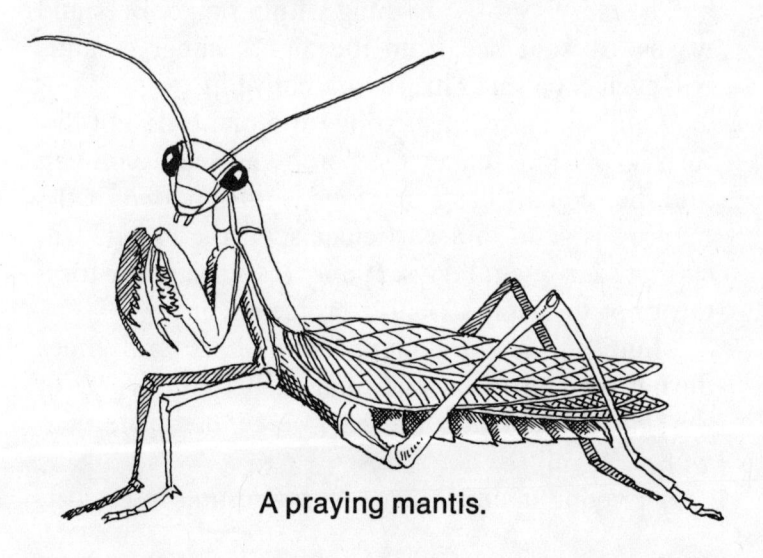

A praying mantis.

The eggs are laid in the fall. The female chooses a twig or weed and lays the eggs inside a frothy egg case. The case hardens, providing a secure winter shelter. The baby mantises emerge in early summer and quickly struggle to leave their winter home. They have to be quick because these little creatures are already killers, and the slow ones provide the first breakfast for their stronger brothers and sisters.

The mantis, unlike the ground beetle, does not run about searching for its food. Instead, it sits quietly on a leaf or twig, its huge front legs folded in prayerful pose. Suddenly, these legs dart out and grasp a passing butterfly. The butterfly is held tight, caught by the toothlike spines on the strong front legs. Still holding the struggling butterfly, the mantis proceeds to devour it alive. Then it cleans itself tidily and, folding its huge legs, waits for its next victim.

The mantis grabs anything within range. Bees and wasps are snatched from the air. A hungry mantis will even eat a small lizard or a baby bird.

If you find a mantis sitting on a plant, do not disturb it, but look under the perch and see if you can find the remains of its previous victims. Often, if the hunting is good in a particular spot, the mantis will sit there for several days. It may then disappear for a day or so to cast its skin in a protected place.

Mantises, like grasshoppers, molt several times during their growth. The final molt occurs early in the fall and the adult insects emerge, complete with wings.

A praying mantis makes an interesting insect pet.

You might be able to get one to perch quietly on a curtain and keep your house free from flies in the summertime, but your mother would probably prefer to see it in a cage.

A mantis cage needs to be fairly roomy. An empty aquarium covered with a screen makes a good home. You should put a twig in for a perch. Praying mantises do not eat plants, so you can use a plastic plant; it would look decorative but would not require any care. Leave the floor of the cage bare so that the food you provide for your mantis cannot escape by burrowing into the sand or soil.

If you have watched a praying mantis outside, you will realize that feeding your insect will be quite a challenging job. You probably do not have the deadly aim of a mantis when it comes to catching a fly on the wing. However, there is a wide variety to offer it—grasshoppers, moths, flies, beetles, and so forth.

You could rear fruit flies and have a continuous supply of live food on hand. Fruit flies are attracted to overripe fruit. You can trap some in a small jar, using a ripe banana as bait. Make a paper funnel with a hole in the bottom to fit the mouth of the jar. This allows the small flies to enter but makes it hard for them to escape. When you have trapped a number of flies, replace the funnel with a plug of cotton. The flies will lay eggs in the banana and in 2 or 3 days the larvae will hatch.

Do not forget to water the mantis cage, even if you are using plastic plants. Your mantis will need a

82 • EXPLORING THE INSECT WORLD

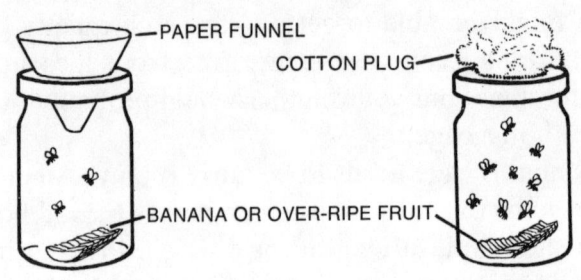

A jar for trapping and raising fruit flies.

lot of water. It will drink droplets scattered on the foliage and glass sides of the cage. It might even learn to drink from an eyedropper or spoon.

The mantis has a small, triangular head and can move it freely sideways, and up and down. It can look over its shoulder, staring at you with large, inquisitive eyes. You will find it makes a good pet because it seems to have more personality than other insects.

The ladybird

Compared to a mantis, a ladybird is a harmless-looking creature, but if you happened to be an aphid you would see it differently. Ladybird eggs are often laid in the middle of an aphid colony. The young hatch, surrounded by their favorite food. All through their larval stages, they eat aphids, and, when they become adults, they go right on eating aphids.

How many aphids can a ladybird eat?

You can try to find out. Put a ladybird beetle in a jar, with a piece of damp paper towel to keep the air humid. Then find a leaf with a colony of aphids on it. Use a fine brush to knock off all but ten aphids. Put the leaf with the aphids in the jar. On the following day, check and see how many aphids have been eaten. See that you do not count cast skins as dead aphids. Then put in a fresh leaf with ten more aphids. If your ladybird always eats all ten aphids, try giving it more each day.

You could also try feeding the larvae of ladybirds. Look for very small larvae, or even eggs, and see how their appetites increase as they grow bigger. You remember that caterpillars stopped feeding just before molting. You will find that your ladybird larvae do this, too.

What happens if your larvae do not get quite enough to eat? If you keep your larvae on a starvation diet, does it take them longer to grow into adults or do they turn into undersized adults?

When you are looking for aphid colonies, you will find other predators as well as ladybirds. The larva of the hover fly is a sluglike creature that slides over the leaf on a trail of saliva. It seizes an aphid with its mouth and sucks out the inside, leaving only the dry skin.

Another aphid eater is the lacewing. It is a delicate, pale green insect with golden eyes, and it does not look like a predator at all. The larvae of some kinds of lacewings have a strange way of protecting themselves from their enemies while they hunt down aphids. They camouflage themselves by carrying bits and pieces of dead aphid skins on their backs. If you find one of these larvae, carefully strip off this debris and put the larva and the dead skins in a jar. You will be able to see there are rows of hooked bristles down its back. The larva may replace the camouflage while you watch.

The parasites

In an aphid colony, you often will find light brown, dead aphids stuck to the leaf. They have been attacked by parasites and are called *mummies*. A tiny wasp lays its eggs in the aphid, and the wasp larva develops inside the aphid. If you cannot see a hole in the mummy, then put it in a jar and wait for the wasp to come out.

You may already have met other parasites if you have reared caterpillars. It is disappointing to watch a caterpillar turn into a pupa, and then, instead of a moth or butterfly, to find some inconspicuous flies or wasps emerge. Sometimes, the caterpillar does not live to form a pupa, and the parasites emerge from its wasted body. But these insects have their place, too. They may not be as pretty to look at, but they do help to control the large numbers of plant eaters.

The ichneumen wasp is a fierce-looking creature with a very slender waist and what appears to be an incredibly long stinger. However, you do not need to fear this stinger—unless you are a caterpillar. The stinger is really an *ovipositor,* or egg-laying tool.

Some types of ichneumen can locate a sawfly larva inside a tree. The ichneumen drills into the wood with its ovipositor, finds the larva, and lays its eggs within the soft body.

If you are ever lucky enough to see a parasite laying its eggs in a caterpillar, you will notice that the caterpillar reacts with alarm when the parasite closes in. Once the eggs are laid and the parasite flies off, the caterpillar goes back to eating, imagining the danger is past. But the caterpillar is doomed. The eggs inside hatch, and the caterpillar continues to eat to feed the unwanted guests.

Garbage disposals

There are insects that are not particular what they eat—fresh or decayed plants, live or dead insects. They are nature's recycling agents.

Among these insects is the earwig. The earwig always seems a rather lowly creature, with its habit of hiding in holes and crawling into cracks. Scientists call this need to be squeezed against a surface *thigmotaxis* or *stereotaxis*. If you put an earwig in a jam jar, you will find that it squeezes itself against the bottom and side of the jar, so that its body curves with the curve of the jar. Even if you shine a light, it will remain still, although earwigs normally run away from light.

It is very rare to see an earwig fly, but they do have wings. They fold them up like a fan and tuck them under the wing cases.

Earwigs spend the winter as adults. You can tell the males and females apart by the shape of their pincers. Those of the male are curved, while the female's are nearly straight. The female lays her eggs in early spring in a hollow she has scooped out of the soil. She watches over the eggs until they hatch and stays with the young for a short time afterward.

You could try rearing earwigs in a glass jar or a fish bowl and see if you can observe the mother earwig with her young. Place a layer of potting soil in the bottom of the jar and scatter some grass seed on it. Earwigs will eat a variety of food—even a little dog food will do.

The earwig's care for her young is interesting because it is the first step toward developing the social way of living found in bees and ants. We will meet them in the next chapters.

CHAPTER 9

The House Builders —Bees and Wasps

ALMOST ALL the insects we have met take no care of their young beyond laying their eggs in the right place. Honeybees are different. They provide their larvae with neat, six-sided homes, and feed them and clean them. If the larva is going to grow up to be a queen, she is treated royally. She is given a larger home and richer food.

Honeybees are *social* insects. Their lives depend on being part of the group. However, the mother, or queen bee, is not really so very different from other insects. She lays her eggs in the right place and pays no more attention to them. It is the worker bees that look after, and feed, the larvae. They feed the queen, too.

Scientists have been fascinated by bees for many, many years and have found out remarkable facts about them. One of the great puzzles has been, how do bees communicate?

You may have seen bees in a glass-sided "obser-

88 • EXPLORING THE INSECT WORLD

vation hive." They move about restlessly. Sometimes, you can pick out the queen with her longer, more tapered body. The bees seem to be moving at random, and, with everyone walking over and around everyone else, you wonder if they know what they are doing.

A scientist, Karl von Frisch, found that bees actually pass information to each other by the way they move about. He called their movements *bee dances*.

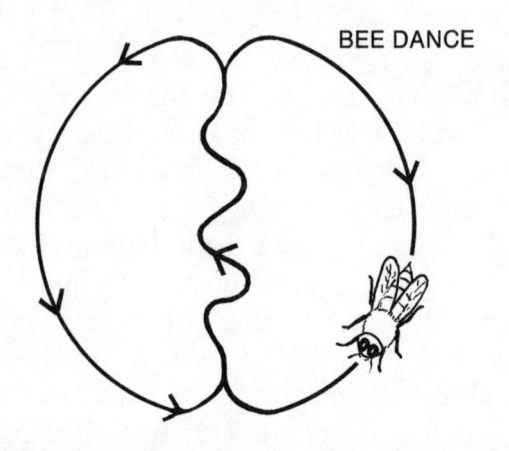

BEE DANCE

These dances are performed by bees returning to the hive from a food-gathering expedition. If the food is near to the hive, the bee does a quick, excited dance. If it is far away, the bee dances more slowly.

The movements of the bee trace out a figure eight, and the diameter of the figure tells the other bees the direction they should take to find food.

These dances are usually performed in the darkness of the hive; the other bees follow the movements by touching the dancing bee with their antennae. Sometimes, however, you can see bees dancing on the entrance to the hive.

If you know a beekeeper, you may be able to sit by a hive and watch the bees returning with their pollen and nectar. It is easy to spot bees returning with pollen because it is carried on their pollen-basket legs. Do any of them dance before going into the hive?

On a warm evening, you may see bees stationed at the doorway, whirring their wings, to keep the air in the hive moving. This helps evaporate the water from the nectar to make rich honey.

Some bees are more placid and easygoing than others, so it is best to know your bees and beekeeper before you get too close to the hive.

Training bees

You can train bees to come to a dish of honey or syrup made from sugar and water. First, put out a square of blue paper smeared with honey in an area where bees are foraging. After bees visit your paper, you can replace it with another square of blue paper. This time put the honey or syrup in a dish in the middle of the paper.

Sometimes, it is hard to get the first bees to visit the honey paper. You might put a drop of honey on the end of a plastic knitting needle and see if you can coax the bee onto the needle. You then carry it over to the honey paper. If the bee circles the paper as it flies off, the chances are that it is memorizing the site, and will be back.

90 • EXPLORING THE INSECT WORLD

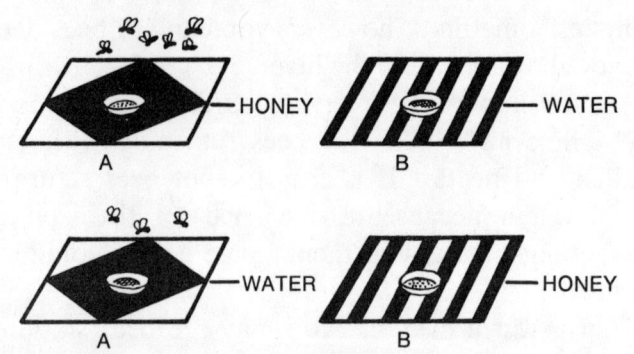

A method for showing that bees recognize patterns. They return to a pattern which had honey even after the honey is replaced with a dish of water.

When you have a number of bees visiting your paper, you can mark them with a dab of paint on the thorax. Do the marked bees come back? How long do they continue to come back?

Do you think that the blue square helps the bees recognize the location of the honey? Try putting a honey dish on a square of red paper and moving the blue paper with its honey 1 or 2 yards away. Do bees come to the red paper, or the blue? Suppose you put only water in the blue-papered dish and honey in the red. Do the bees come to the red or the blue?

Scientists have studied bees' color vision for many years. They reasoned that bees must see in color to explain the colorful petals of flowers. The markings in the middle of flowers would seem to guide the bees to the nectaries and, while reaching down into the flowers, they transfer the pollen from one flower to the next.

When scientists studied the way bees respond to color, using feeding dishes on colored cards, the results were not always what they expected. They also placed the dishes on bands of colored light to get purer colors.

Bees see in color, but they do not have the same range of color vision as we do. They do not see red as a color, but they do see ultraviolet, which we do not. A flower garden viewed through a bee's eyes would be a vastly different place. The leaves and stems of the plants would be shades of gray and black. The flowers would be bright against that dull background. Many of the white flowers would appear to be blue-green, and there would be markings in the centers of some flowers that we would not see.

It was found that bees could be trained to recognize shapes as well as colors. But their ability to do this is very limited. They cannot tell a square from a circle or a triangle, but they can learn to tell a very irregular shape with a broken outline from a smooth outline, such as a circle.

You can try to replace the color cards at your feeding stations with shapes and see if you can train your bees to recognize them.

Will bees come to artificial sweeteners? We use all sorts of low-calorie sweeteners. Make a solution of sweetener and water that tastes to you as sweet as a solution of sugar and water. Place the two dishes side by side on your feeding station. Do as many bees drink from the low-calorie dish as from the other?

92 • EXPLORING THE INSECT WORLD

Bees need water in hot weather. Sometimes, you see bees lapping at a puddle or at a damp place at the edge of a stream. Often, the same drinking place is used by bees summer after summer.

Bees can apparently detect water without touching it. You can show this at your feeding station if you replace your dish of honey with a jar of water

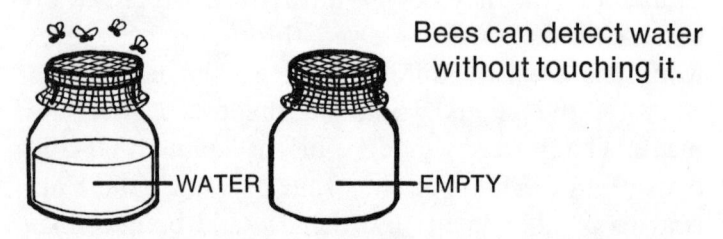

Bees can detect water without touching it.

WATER — EMPTY

on a very hot afternoon. Fill the jar half full and cover it with window screening. Put another jar near it, but without water. You will find that bees hover over the jar with water in it, but ignore the other.

Another interesting fact, discovered by using a feeding station, is that bees have a sense of time. They have an inner clock that prompts them to do things at the same time each day. Set out food for 2 hours each day, at the same time, over a period of several days. Mark the bees that visit the food. The next day, put food out much earlier, and leave it out all day. The marked bees should start coming to the table at about the time they were fed on the previous days.

Wasps

Your feeding station may attract wasps as well as

bees, but you will find that they cannot be trained to come regularly to the honey. Wasps have a more varied diet than bees and will eat, and feed their young, meat as well as nectar.

Many wasps, too, live in communal homes. Some make their homes from paper. They manufacture paper from wood fiber, just as we do. You can sometimes see a wasp scraping wood from a weathered fence post or a dead tree. Look for the tiny scratches it makes on the wood. The wasp chews the wood into a pulp and processes it into paper that it adds to the nest.

As the nights begin to get cold in the fall, life in the wasps' nest slows down. The young queens mate and then look for a safe place to spend the winter. The workers and the drones all die. So, if you find a wasps' nest late in the fall, or a last year's one, you can take it apart and examine the tough paper walls and the tiers of six-sided cells which serve as homes for the larvae.

Solitary bees and wasps

Not all bees and wasps live in hives and nests. Those that live alone are called *solitary* bees or wasps. You may be surprised to learn that there are far more kinds of solitary bees and wasps than social ones.

Often, great numbers of solitary bees make their homes close to each other, but they all live independently of each other.

Many of the solitary bees and wasps make their

homes in hollow stems or small burrows. A good example is the leaf-cutting bee. You can see where a leaf-cutting bee has been at work if you find plants that have neat, oval or round pieces cut from the leaves and petals. The bee alights on the plant and, holding the leaf between its legs, speedily cuts a disc with its jaws, and flies off. Soon it will be back for another piece.

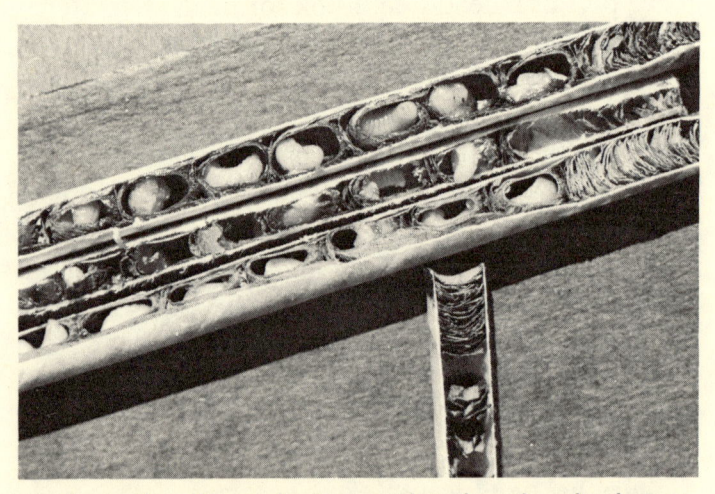

A section through straws showing developing larvae of the leaf-cutter bee.

If you could follow the bee, you would find that it disappears into a small hole or hollow stem. This is its nest. It carefully lays overlapping pieces of leaf to form the lining of a thimble-shaped cell. Then it stores a food supply of nectar and pollen and lays an egg on this. The cell is sealed off with round discs of leaf, and another cell is made on top of the first.

THE HOUSE BUILDERS—BEES AND WASPS • 95

When the tube of cells is completed, the mother bee flies off, leaving the young to look out for themselves.

Solitary wasps also provide food for their larvae. They leave a supply of fresh meat. When the wasp has selected, or made, her burrow, she goes off in search of food. Some wasps look for a spider, others a caterpillar. She stings and paralyzes, but does not kill, the victim. She takes it back to the nest and lays an egg on it. When the egg hatches, the larva will have a supply of fresh meat.

The French naturalist, Jean Henri Fabre, studied the habits of a solitary wasp, called *Sphex*. This wasp gives a grasshopper to its young for food. Fabre marveled at the careful way *Sphex* paralyzed the grasshopper—as precise as the work of a nerve surgeon.

Then Fabre tried some simple experiments which showed that *Sphex* follows a pattern of behavior that has been laid down during the long years of its evolution. Faced with a new problem, it cannot respond with a new set of actions to solve it—or even change its usual set of actions.

Sphex drags the grasshopper to its burrow by an antenna, so Fabre cut off the antennae. *Sphex* dragged it by a palp. Fabre cut off the palps. *Sphex* then tried, opening its jaws wide, to grab the grasshopper by the head. Fabre tried to get the wasp to grasp the grasshopper by a leg, or by the ovipositor, but it would not do so. The *Sphex* always pulls its victim into its burrow head first, and this wasp was not going to try anything different.

On another occasion, Fabre waited until the wasp

had dragged a grasshopper into the tunnel and laid an egg on it. It only had to seal off the tunnel and the job was finished. Fabre removed the grasshopper without disturbing the tunnel. The wasp hurried in and inspected the empty nest. It spent some time there and then went ahead and closed the entrance, packing together grains of sand to build a strong wall. It would then go off and dig another tunnel, catch another grasshopper, lay another egg, and build another wall. It had to complete the whole sequence of acts and, even though the nest was empty, it sealed it off with care.

Making your own nests

Sometimes, you can attract solitary bees and wasps to artificial nests. All you need to do is to set out blocks of wood with holes drilled in them. Try a hole in the range of ¼ to ½ an inch. Another way you can make a nest is by cutting a carton of milk straws in half and gluing them in place.

Put your nests in a variety of places with the tunnels lying horizontally. Tie them to a branch or lay them on a window sill. Set them in the sun and in the shade.

You may find that other creatures use the holes as a hiding place. Make a list of the kinds of insects which find their way into your nesting holes.

If you are lucky and a bee or wasp occupies a hole, then you can keep records of its activity. How often does it visit the nest? How long is it away from the nest, and what does it bring back? What happens

THE HOUSE BUILDERS—BEES AND WASPS

if you move the nesting block a few inches while the insect is gone? What happens if you block the door before the nest is complete?

Still another kind of nest can be made by cutting a groove in a block of wood and then laying another piece on top. Fasten the blocks together with rubber bands.

This type of nest allows you to look into the nest by carefully taking the blocks of wood apart. You will see the individual cells and developing larvae. If the nest is newly completed, you will need a lens to see the tiny grub. Can you see the larva's food supply? If it is a wasp, how many caterpillars or spiders are there in each cell? Can you see any sign of life in the paralyzed victims? Are they really being eaten alive?

It usually takes from 1 to 4 weeks for the larvae to develop into pupae. In the case of wasps, the adults chew their way out of the cell about 3 weeks later. Bees, however, may remain in the cocoon till the following spring. In this way, the new adults emerge when the flowers they need are in bloom and there will be a supply of pollen to feed to their young. Often, one species of bee uses the pollen from one species of plant.

These solitary bees are important pollinators, too, and you will read in the last chapter that some farmers have domesticated the solitary bee.

CHAPTER 10

The City Builders —Ants

THE ANT does not appear to be an insect that would be the winner of the insect success story. Its body is so clearly divided into three parts that you wonder what holds it together. Its head looks too big, but its brain is tiny. Most ants have lost the wings that give insects such an advantage over other creatures. They are restricted to life on, and under, the ground.

Yet ants have crawled over the ground unchanged for 70 million years. They live in every kind of place you can think of. There are ants' nests under busy sidewalks and in remote deserts. They eat a great variety of food. Some kinds of tropical ants have adapted to living in the heated houses of cooler climates where they find year-round warmth and food as well. Ants make use of plants and other creatures in a way that is only equaled by man.

Ants live longer than many other insects. Workers may live for 3 years, and queens have been known to live for as long as 20 years.

But the ant has paid a penalty for its success. An ant cannot live by itself. It is only a little part of a large ant family, and it can have no life apart from the family.

There is one time when this rule is broken and an ant does live alone. That is when the queen is starting a new nest.

You may have seen the first stages of the ant's story if you have watched a cloud of flying ants on a calm summer evening. These winged ants are males and females and one evening, when the weather is right, they fly from their nests and mate in the air. After this brief, adventurous flight, the male dies, or is eaten by predators, and those females that escape the same fate alight on the ground.

The newly mated queen then does a strange thing. You can often watch this when there are swarms of flying ants about. She tears off her wings or rubs against a stone until they fall off. It seems a drastic step, but she will have no use for wings in her underground home. The large muscles which worked the wings will be absorbed as food in the hungry days ahead.

The queen digs out a little hole in the earth and burrows into the ground. Here she lays her eggs and tends them. She sometimes has to eat some to keep up her strength, and, when the eggs hatch into larvae, she may give them eggs to eat. When at last these larvae develop into ants, they go off in search of food. They can now take over the jobs of looking after the young and feeding the queen. The queen is

REPLETE HONEY POT ANTS

DRIVER ANTS

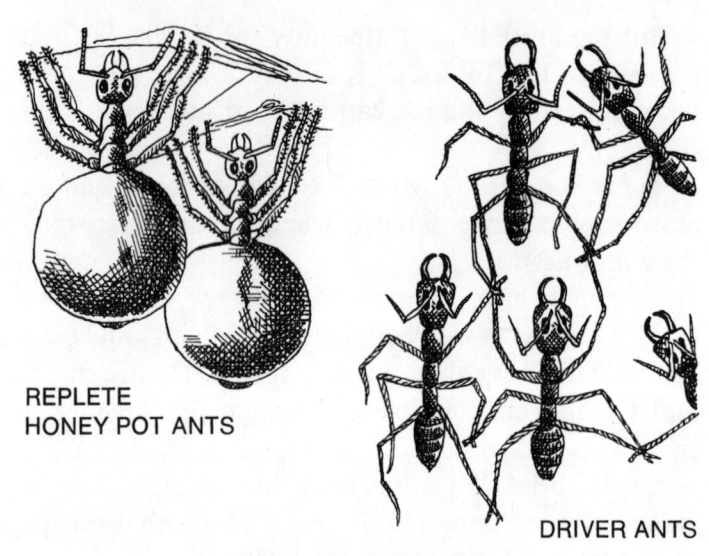

Ants have specific jobs.

no longer alone, and neither she nor her children can live by themselves.

Because ants have adopted the social way of life, they have been able to develop very complex habits that are not shared by other insects. Ants have not learned to make wax or paper for building materials as bees and wasps do. Instead, they use members of their own colony for all sorts of special jobs.

There are ants in some colonies with cork-shaped heads; their job is to act as doorkeepers, stopping up the door holes. There are ants in another colony which are used as storage jars. They are pumped full of nectar, just as bees fill wax cells. These ants live in the sandy soil of the desert. The nectar-bearing flowers they feed on bloom for only a short time.

THE CITY BUILDERS—ANTS • 101

WEAVER ANTS

ANT TENDING APHIDS

PARASOL ANT

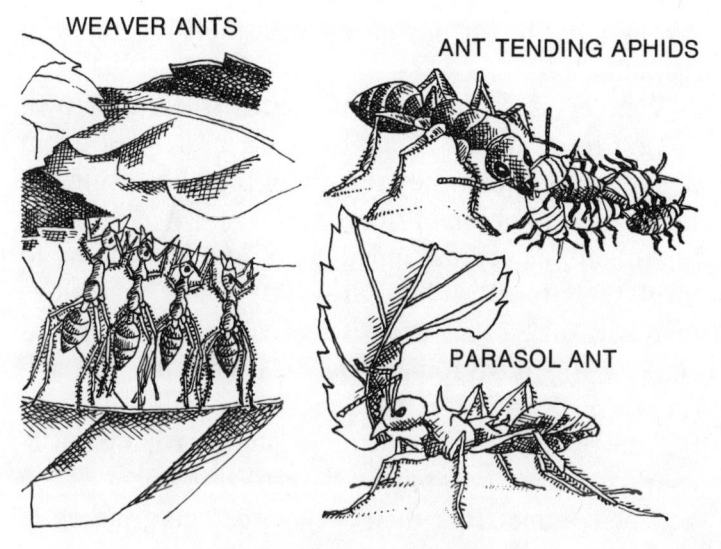

Ants act as a colony.

They must store food for the long periods of drought. They do this by using members of their own colony as "honey pots." These living honey pots are called *repletes* (meaning full) and spend their whole life hanging from the ceiling of the storage vault. The workers bring in nectar and feed them. Their stomachs swell, and there they hang—like golden grapes —full of honey to be shared during the hungry days.

The blind driver ants of the tropics do not build a home but use their own bodies, tangled together, to form a hollow ball. In the middle of this living nest, the queen lays her eggs and tiny workers tend them. At regular intervals, the nest breaks up, and the ants go on the march. The whole army of ants—100,000 workers carrying the queen and the young—files through the forest devouring the small creatures in its path.

Weaver ants have turned members of their own colony into "tools." They live in a nest made from pockets of leaves. They sew these together using the larvae like a bobbin of silk.

Ants may even use members of another colony to meet their needs. There are some kinds that wage war and take other species to live in their nests as slaves. Ants have found ways to use plants and animals.

The parasol ants tend huge, underground mushroom gardens, weeding and fertilizing them. They get their name from their way of carrying pieces of leaf back to their nest to make a compost on which to grow their mold. When a queen starts a new colony, she carries with her some fungus to start her new garden.

As well as ants that tend gardens, there are ants that have their own "domestic animals." These you can watch because this farming is often done outside the nest. The ants' cows are aphids. These little plant suckers are greedy creatures and suck more sap from the plant than they need. The extra passes through as a droplet of sticky honeydew. This is what attracts the ants.

Often, the ant strokes the aphid with its antennae. The aphid seems to like this and gives off more honeydew. Mark some of the ants tending the aphids so that you can recognize them again. You can do this with a fine brush and some quick-drying enamel paint. Mark the ant on its thorax. Now you can tell if the same group of ants is visiting the aphids or if they come at random.

You may be able to see the earth shelters that the ants sometimes make around low plants to protect the aphids. Try prying some of the aphids loose so that they are no longer feeding. How do the ants treat them?

Ant-watching

There is a lot you can learn about ants just by watching them outdoors or in an artificial nest. Two of the most puzzling things about ants in a colony are how they communicate with each other and how each knows its own job.

Start ant-watching close to a nest where there are a lot of ants hurrying about. Mark an ant and pin a dead fly in the path of the marked ant. Does the ant go to the nest for help? Does it lead ants back to the food or has it "told" the others where to find food? Now take a bigger piece of food, such as a caterpillar, and divide it into two pieces—one bigger than the other. Pin each in the path of ants looking for food. Do the same number of ants come from the nest to each bit of food or do more ants come to the larger piece? Do ants follow the same route out from the nest to the food as they do on the homeward journey?

One way an ant can give another ant directions is by leaving a scent trail. The ant presses its body against the ground and leaves a slight smell that an-

104 • EXPLORING THE INSECT WORLD

other ant can follow. Ants use their "feelers" to detect this smell. Scientists have found they can make an artificial trail using formic acid. Another way to make an artificial trail is with the body of a freshly killed ant.

Rub your finger across an ant road and watch how the ants react when they come to that place. Another way you can investigate an ant trail is by placing a sheet of paper so that the ants cross it to a piece of food. Then turn the paper to a different angle (*see* diagram). Do the next ants that come along cross directly to the food or do they follow the trail to the edge of the paper? Try placing food on a piece of paper and waiting for some ants to find it.

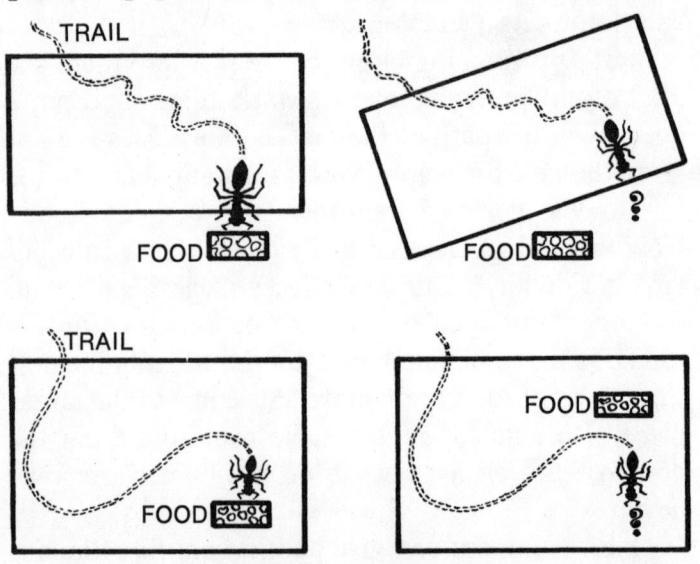

An ant will follow his own trail to food rather than go directly to the food.

Now move the food to another part of the paper (*see diagram*). Do late arrivals go to the food in its new place or do they go where the food was before you moved it? In other words, are the ants attracted to the food itself or are they following a trail that has been left for them?

Making a nest

In order to learn more about ants and their ways, you can keep them indoors in an artificial nest. You can buy an "ant farm" in a pet shop or a variety store, or you can make your own.

The simplest type of nest is made in a glass jar. Fill the jar with damp sand and set it in a pan of water so that the ants cannot escape (like a castle

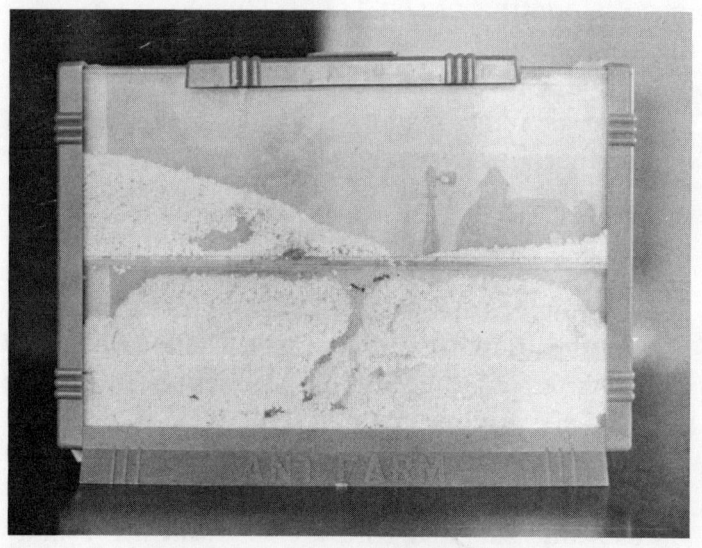

An ant farm, showing ants at work.

surrounded by a moat). On top of the jar put a piece of cardboard with a small hole in it. This is the feeding station. You can seal it in place with a ring of modeling clay around the top of the jar. The ants will come up from the nest in the sand to forage for food just as they do outside.

You can easily find a few ants to live in your jar, but these would be workers. To keep your colony going, you need a queen and finding a queen is not easy. Try digging into a nest. As you dig, the disturbed queens go deeper into tunnels. You can recognize the queens by their size. They are bigger and, often, shinier than the workers. Have a plastic bag or jar ready for your ants and, if you miss the queen, take a selection of workers, larvae, and pupae. Before trying to put your catch into its new nest, it is a good idea to put the bag or jar of ants in the refrigerator for an hour so that the ants are less active and, therefore, easier to handle.

Another way you might try to colonize your jar or ant farm is to leave it, with food in it, at the entrance to an ants' nest for a day. The ants will make trails to the food. Then leave a hose gently running long enough to flood the ant colony. The ants will follow the trails to your jar. Some ants will arrive carrying pupae, some with larvae, and when you see a queen arrive, you can turn off the hose.

The tiny black garden ants are the best ones to collect. Fire ants sting, and some ants bite.

The ants supplied with an ant farm are usually harvester ants and are all workers.

THE CITY BUILDERS—ANTS • 107

A more elaborate nest can be made from plaster of Paris. The ants live in tunnels in the plaster block. To make this type of nest, you will need a shoebox lid and a piece of glass that is about 1 inch narrower than the lid and ½ inch shorter. Lay the glass so that one end of the glass touches the edge of the lid and there is a ½-inch margin on each of the other three sides.

Now you design your tunnels, using modeling clay. Make a big chamber close to the end where the glass does not touch the lid and several smaller chambers, all connected with passageways (*see* photograph). Over this, you pour the plaster of Paris and

A plaster-of-Paris ant nest, showing a clay model and final nest.

allow it to harden. When you remove the box and the modeling clay, you will have a plaster nest with a glass lid.

When you first introduce the ants, put them in the large chamber. Then lay a sheet of cardboard over the tunnels and the ants will make their home in the

Ants living in an ant nest.

dark. The large chamber becomes their foraging area. You can slide the lid off far enough to allow you to give them food without disturbing the nest.

Whatever type of nest you use, you will need to give your ants water. Add a few drops each day to the sand or plaster. Do not feed your ants more than about twice a week. Uneaten food will get moldy and can kill the colony. Honey, peanut butter, tiny bits of fruit, hamburger, or a dead fly make fine meals for your ants. You can test other food to find what they like.

You can use the jar nest to try some feeding investigations with your ants. You can, of course, watch how they react to different types of food. Or you can make separate feeding stations and see if

THE CITY BUILDERS—ANTS • *109*

ants are more attracted to some foods than to others. The author used "Tinkertoy" rods to connect the small feeding stations to the main nest (sketch).

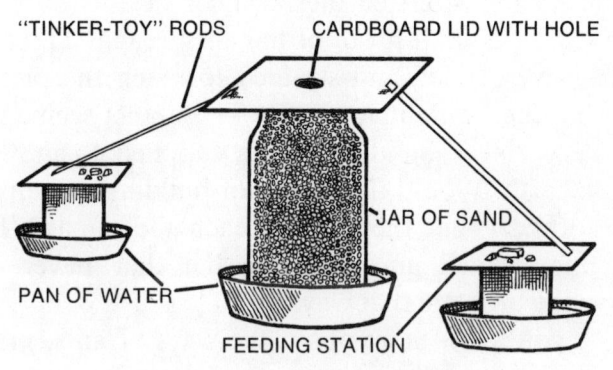

An easy-to-make ant nest.

They have notched ends which clip easily onto the cardboard. You can fasten the rod at the other end with modeling clay. How long do the ants keep coming to the feeding station after you have wiped it clean?

Color a drop of honey with blue food coloring and allow only one or two ants to feed on it. If they are light-colored ants, you will be able to see the blue honey in their stomachs. Now remove the honey. After awhile, you will find that most of the ants are dyed blue. What does this tell you about the feeding habits of ants?

Use a magnifying lens to watch how ants tear a piece of food apart. Notice the way their jaws work, and how large a piece an ant can carry.

If you introduce an ant from another nest to your colony, what sort of welcome does it get? If you take an ant out of your colony for a few days and then return it, do the ants treat it as an intruder?

One scientist tested the behavior of ants by placing some pupae just out of the ants' reach. The ants were very excited and strained to reach the pupae, waving their antennae wildly. These ants seemed to be very clever builders, so he supplied them with loose earth. Would they think of building a ramp or platform so that they could reach the pupae? The scientist waited and watched, but they never did solve the problem that way.

As you learn more about the ways of ants, many questions about their behavior will occur to you. See if you can answer your own questions by watching and experimenting.

CHAPTER 11

Exploring a Pond

UNDER THE STILL surface of a pond, hidden from curious eyes, is the ruthless world of the hunter and the hunted. A huge dragonfly nymph lurks in the weeds and, with deadly aim, catches a young mayfly for dinner. A large beetle swims down from the surface, with its oxygen supply tucked under its wings, and seizes a midge larva as it loops its way through the gloom.

In almost any stream or pond, you can find some of the insects mentioned in the following pages. So gather up some equipment, find a stretch of water, and meet the inhabitants.

Equipment

An effective tool for catching water insects is a kitchen sieve tied to a long stick. You will also need a light-colored pan so you can examine your catch. It is a good idea to have several jars along so you can separate different kinds of insects.

An eyedropper and a pair of tweezers are both

useful for transferring animals from the pan to jars. A basting tube (which looks like an oversized eyedropper) is another handy tool. You can use it to wash out your sieve in your pan or for drawing water out of the pan if it is too deep. Sometimes, you will use it for catching insects.

An important part of your equipment is a notebook and pencil. Make a note of "what," and "where," and "when." Your notebook can remind you where you found some interesting specimens and can help you follow the changes through the seasons.

The water's surface

Even within the one pond there are a lot of different *habitats,* or places to live. The first place to look for insects is right on the surface.

The commonest surface dweller is the water strider. It has a slender body, up to ½ inch long, and skates about on two pairs of legs—the middle and hind pair. The short front legs are used for seizing and holding food.

An insect that lives on the surface of the pond does not have any problem breathing. But it does have to have some adaptations to live there.

If you look closely at a water strider you will see that its feet dent the surface of the water. Water has a very thin elastic skin—a skin that is surprisingly strong. You can prove this for yourself by floating a dry needle in a dish of water. However, if the needle breaks through the surface film and becomes wet, then it will sink.

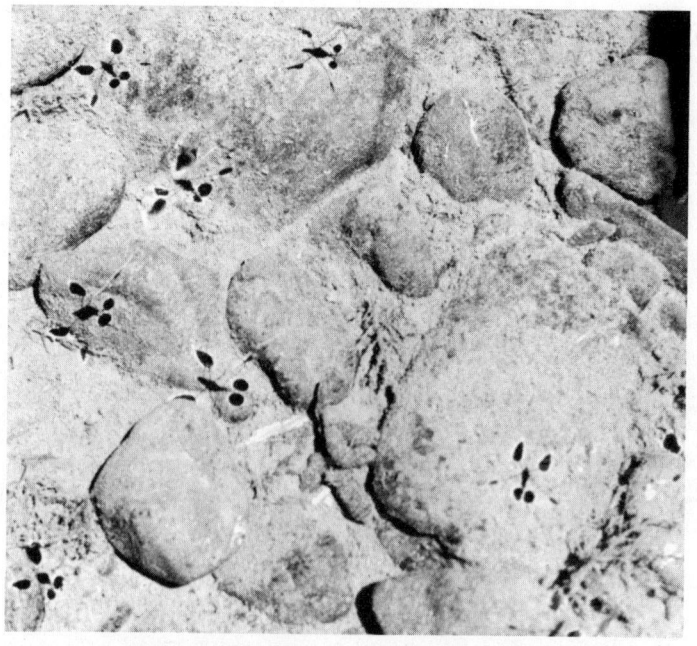

Shadows cast by water striders.

The same thing would happen to the water strider, so it has a coating of velvetlike hair that does not wet easily. Even its feet end in a tuft of hairs, and it walks lightly on the film rather as a man in snowshoes walking over the snow.

Water striders can be kept in an aquarium, but you would need to cover it with cheesecloth as some can fly—and they are all strong jumpers. Also, it is best to carry them home, either dry, or in damp moss. If you try to take them home in a jar of water, the splashing water will cause the insects to sink and drown.

The water strider lays its eggs on floating pond plants. The eggs hatch in about 2 weeks, and the little water striders are quite similar to the adults. They go through five molts before becoming adults. See if you can find young water striders. Can you see any difference between the young and adults?

Water striders feed on dead or live insects that have fallen onto and are trapped in the surface film. Try feeding one a live ant. You might even be able to get one to eat a tiny bit of raw meat.

If you add a drop of detergent to water, this destroys the surface film. What would happen to a water strider that was in the neighborhood of a drop of detergent?

Another insect to look for is the whirligig beetle, which leads a dizzy life, spinning round and round on the surface film. The upper half of the beetle repels water, the lower half does not. The result is that the beetle floats at its midline with its back dry. So it lives half in and half out of the water, and, in order to make the best of both worlds, the beetle has divided eyes. The upper half are for seeing in air and the lower half are for seeing in water. (Like the water strider, the whirligig beetle lives on small animals trapped in the surface film.)

Under the surface film

As well as living on the film, there are insects that live under the film, walking on the underside like a fly on the ceiling. This is where you find the larvae of the mosquito, often called *wrigglers*.

There are two common kinds to look for. One hangs head down from the film, with only its breathing tube touching the film. The other lies horizontally below the surface film, and the area carrying the breathing pores breaks through the surface.

Because mosquito larvae breathe at the surface of the water, spreading a very thin film of oil over the pond is an effective way of controlling them. Another method of control, which has less effect on other forms of life in the pond, is to clear away half-submerged vegetation from around the pond. This removes the resting and hiding places of the larvae. Fish and other predators find them easily and reduce their numbers. So you can see that the first step in waging war against an insect is getting to know the enemy!

You will notice that a mosquito larva has no legs. Look carefully, and you will see that it swims tail first.

Can you see how it eats? One kind of mosquito is like a busy housewife cleaning the ceiling with a feather duster. It lives on particles that stick to the surface film, sweeping them to its mouth with its feeding brushes.

A mosquito pupa is rather like a tadpole with its tail curved around its body. Unlike most pupae, it is quite active. Can you see how the pupa breathes? How does it move? If you find a pupa that is straightened out, then it is time for it to emerge as an adult. This only takes a short time. The adult rests on the cast skin before flying off.

Mosquitoes can breed in very small areas of water—temporary puddles that collect in tree trunks, tin cans, or old tires. Try to make a small pond of your own in early summer and see if you can attract mosquitoes to lay eggs in it. Even a small pan makes a good temporary pond. Set it out in a shaded place and fill it with water. Add a few grass clippings for food and shelter. Make observations each day. How long is it before you find insect life in your pond? What stage of insects do you find?

Be sure to empty the pan when adults begin to emerge. You do not want any more mosquitoes in your neighborhood!

An interesting time to follow the colonization of a water area is when the snow melts and "temporary" water areas form. Insects occupy every niche in nature, and these areas of melting snow are no exception. In fact, it is in these that many of the mosquito problems start.

The surface commuters

Deeper in the water of the pond, you will find water boatmen, backswimmers, various water beetles, and water bugs. These all get their oxygen from the air; so, they have to commute to the surface for a fresh supply. Look for the various ways they get their oxygen. Backswimmers carry bubbles of air on their body hairs. There is a beetle that carries a bubble under its wing covers—rather like a diver with an aqualung. The water scorpion has a long tube at the end of its abdomen so that it resembles a swimmer with a snorkel tube.

You will find quite a number of different kinds of water beetles. These are all quite easy to recognize as beetles because they have the hard, shiny wing covers. All beetles do. The young stage, however, is not at all "beetlelike." It is called a water tiger and is one of the fiercest hunters in the pond. It uses its fringed legs like oars and also swims by wriggling movements. If you watch a water tiger eat, you will see that it bites into its prey with strong jaws and holds it until nothing but an empty skin remains. Instead of swallowing its meat and digesting it in its stomach, the water tiger pumps digestive juices into the body of its prey and sucks in a liquid diet.

Try feeding an adult diving beetle in a jar where you can watch it. Does it feed the same way?

The bottom dwellers

There are some young insects that are as much at home underwater as fish. Some of these have developed gills and breathe oxygen that is dissolved in the water. They can live under stones, among plants, or even buried in the mud because they have no need to go to the surface to breathe.

The nymph of the mayfly is a good example of this group. Mayflies eat vegetable material, mostly algae and tiny diatoms. Gently wash some water plants in clear water and see if you can find some of these delicate creatures. They have gills on each side of the body and three long "tails." The gills vibrate, keeping the water moving past the insect. When there is not much oxygen dissolved in the water, the gills work harder in an effort to get more oxygen. Boil some water to drive out the oxygen and then cool it in the refrigerator. Put a mayfly nymph into this oxygen-poor water. Can you see the gill movement speed up?

The nymphs may live underwater for as short a period as 6 weeks, or as long as 2 years. The adult emerges and flies off for a short time. Then it sheds its skin, wings and all. There are new wings underneath. You can sometimes find these fragile, cast skins of the mayfly on the plants beside the stream. No other insect sheds its adult skin in this way. The mayfly does not live long to enjoy its new skin. It mates, lays eggs, and dies in the space of a few hours.

If you are collecting in a pond with a muddy bottom, then you are likely to scoop up the larva of a midge. You will easily recognize it because of its red color. It is often called a bloodworm. This larva, which grows to about ½ inch in length, lives in a tubelike burrow in the mud. If you sift carefully through the mud, you may find some of the tubes made of debris cemented together by saliva.

This blood-red larva is something of a curiosity in the insect world because the red color is due to *hemoglobin* dissolved in the blood—just as we have hemoglobin in our blood. In both cases, it acts as an oxygen carrier and helps the bloodworm to survive in the mud where the oxygen content is low.

Another fly larva that lives in water is the phantom midge. It is not easy to find because it is almost transparent, and only its dark eyes and buoyancy organs show as it hangs motionless in the water.

Two other interesting groups of creatures that you are likely to come across are the dragonflies and caddisflies. You can learn about them in the following chapters.

Your own aquarium

You will probably want to take some pond insects home for awhile and watch how they live. This is not always easy but, if you carry out some of the following suggestions, you should be able to do it.

When you bring home the pond material you can carry it, in water, in securely tied plastic food bags. Oxygen and carbon dioxide can pass through the plastic bag, but you must keep the bags of water cool.

The insects that are completely aquatic depend on the oxygen that is dissolved in the water. In rushing mountain streams, air bubbles get trapped in the water, and this water is high in dissolved oxygen. Here you find insects that need a lot of oxygen. These would soon die if you put them in a jar of still water.

Pond insects get along with a lower amount of oxygen, so are easier to keep in an aquarium. However, you still need to be careful about two things. One is not to let the water get warm, because heating drives out the oxygen. The other is to use a shallow container. This gives a larger surface in contact with the air so that more oxygen is taken into the water. A deep, narrow jar is a sure way to "drown" your insects.

If you have a glass aquarium, it is easier to see

your insects, but even a plastic basin makes a good container. Put in a few water plants. They provide hiding places for the insects, food for the plant eaters, and produce oxygen during the day. Some stones from the pond, covered with slime or algae, will provide food and resting places.

Spend some time watching the insects at the pond to get some clues about what they eat. If you want to learn more about one kind of insect, it is best to rear it alone in the aquarium; to learn about the life-and-death struggle in the pond, include several different species. You might also collect snails and other animals to study how they relate to the insects.

Once again, your notebook is an important tool. Write down a list of the animals you have introduced to your aquarium. Find out which are predators and which are the prey. Do the meat eaters attack each other? Do the prey have any advantages that help them escape—quick movement, camouflage, and so on? Do the predators and prey seem to live in different parts of the aquarium? Do they live among the weeds, or under the stones? And, of course, the final question to answer is: Who survives in this fierce eat-or-be-eaten world?

CHAPTER 12

Dragonflies on Patrol

WHEN YOU VISIT a pond on a summer day you are sure to see the gleam of a dragonfly as it skims over the water, snapping up a mosquito on the wing. Stop and watch the aerial acrobatics as it flies backward, twists and turns, and then stops in midair.

Sometimes, it is the dragonfly's small cousin, the damselfly, that catches your attention. Both insects belong to the same order, called *Odonata,* which means "toothed jaws." When you get better acquainted with a dragonfly and watch it eat, you will agree that this is a good name!

Dragonflies and damselflies can be separated by several features:

Dragonflies rest with their wings spread out like airplanes. Damselflies fold their wings up over their backs.

The hind wings of dragonflies are larger than the front wings. Those of the damselfly are almost the same size.

The veining patterns on the wings are different.

A dragonfly's territory

As you watch a dragonfly, you may see that there is a pattern to its flight. It stays in one area and hovers between short flights. When it rests, it always returns to the same perch, usually a plant sticking out of the water.

This will be a male dragonfly and it is patrolling its territory. It will drive away other males of its own kind. But when a female comes to the territory, the dragonfly mates with her and she lays her eggs there. This means that the eggs are laid in separate areas instead of overcrowding the best sites.

Biologists describe this way of acting as "territorial behavior." Many kinds of birds defend the areas around their nests, driving away members of their own species. But it is unusual for insects to do this.

Hunting dragonflies with a butterfly net.

To take a closer look at a dragonfly, you have to catch it. A good way to do this is to use a net and stalk it while it rests on its perch. You will find that it is hard to catch a dragonfly on the wing.

Left: an aerial net. Right: a water net. Both are used for catching insects.

The net should be light enough for you to be able to move it quickly. The bag should be made of strong nylon net stitched firmly to round a hoop of wire. It should be long enough so that, when the hoop is flipped over, it closes the bag, trapping the insect (*see* photograph). You then hold the insect lightly

A child is taking an insect from the net the correct way.

through the cloth with one hand and reach into the net with a jar in the other hand. You have got it trapped! For collecting nymphs underwater, you need a stronger net or the sieve mentioned in Chapter 11.

In spite of its dazzling beauty in flight, close up the dragonfly is a remarkably ugly creature! It has huge, bulging eyes that almost meet on the top of its head and a mouth that can open as wide as its face. Its legs are grouped just under its chin—a good position for scooping up insects but a poor position for walking. The four clear wings are attached to powerful flight muscles. The veins give the fragile-looking wings strength. Can you see how the veins are arranged to give the wings extra strength at the front edge?

If you mark the dragonfly with a dab of paint on its thorax, you will be able to recognize it again. Now you can find out some things about dragonfly behavior with no more equipment than sharp eyes and a notebook to write down what you see. For example, does the marked dragonfly patrol the same area each day?

Try and catch another dragonfly from a nearby territory of the same species as the one you are watching; release it in the area. The first dragonfly will try to drive the invader out of its territory. Does it just put on a show of being fierce or do they actually fight?

Can you see the "limits" of the territory? Quite often, the boundaries are marked by a clump of plants, or a tree, or a projecting shoreline. What would happen if you covered the boundary marker with a piece of sheet, or your jacket, to hide it from the dragonfly? What would happen if you removed the dragonfly's perch? Do you think the dragonfly depends mostly on its eyesight?

Different species of dragonflies sometimes have overlapping territories. They do not interfere with each other because they patrol at different heights. You find damselflies skimming over the water and perching on a low weed. Middle-sized dragonflies fly a few feet above the water, while the largest ones patrol well over your head and may perch in a nearby tree.

Life underwater

Most people know the adult dragonfly, but few know its young. You might guess, from where the female lays her eggs, that the young stages are spent underwater. Even with that clue, you would have trouble recognizing the young nymph. It is a drab-colored insect, with a short, squat body. Like the adult, it has large eyes and a big appetite.

To find the nymphs, look on underwater plants, or on sunken logs, or in the mud at the bottom of a pond. Scooping up the mud in a kitchen strainer is a good way to find them. You may come across the nymphs of a damselfly, too. They have slender bodies and three flattened "tails." These are actually the gills for breathing underwater.

The dragonfly nymph also has gills. They consist of branching air tubes in the abdomen. Water, containing dissolved oxygen, is drawn into the *rectum* at the rear of the body. If you place a nymph in a shallow dish of water and look closely, you will notice pulsing movements of the abdomen as it breathes.

It can also use this breathing system for moving. Put a drop of food color behind the nymph. Then touch it suddenly on the back with a toothpick. Can you see the nymph draw water into the rectum and then expel it—to "jet propel" itself through the wa-

Children collecting insects at a stream.

ter? Compare this with the way a damselfly moves. Notice how the damselfly uses its whole body.

Next, see if you can persuade your dragonfly to eat. If it is really hungry, it may take a tiny piece of hamburger or a dead fly from the end of a toothpick. Twirl the toothpick in the water with the meat close to the nymph's mouth. Can you see how its grabs the meat?

The nymph has a very strange lower lip, or labium. It is almost like an arm with grasping hooks at its end. When not in use, the labium folds up beneath the nymph's face. With a toothpick, you can gently

LABIUM

LABIUM IN AN EXTENDED POSITION

A dragonfly nymph has a labium.

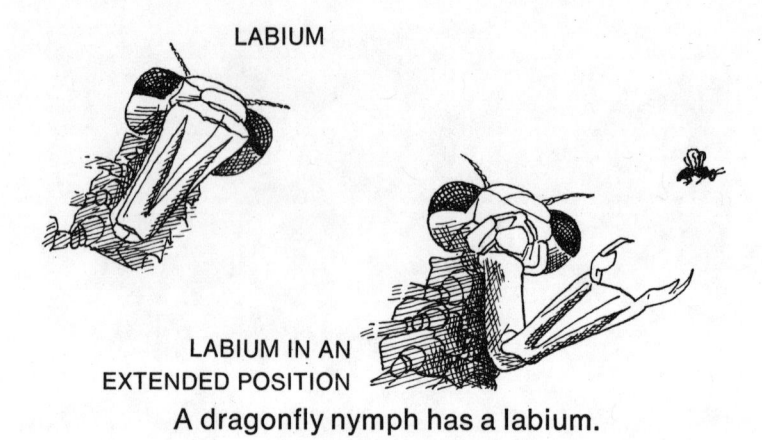

pull out this strange structure and look at it. When a victim is near, the labium shoots out and impales it on the hooks. Then it brings the food back within reach of the powerful jaws. The labium also serves as a saucer to catch the crumbs.

As the nymph grows, it casts its skin. It molts up to ten times before it is fully grown and, with each molt, small changes take place. When the insect is close to being an adult, you can see the wing pads on its back.

If you find a nymph with well-developed wing pads, you can keep it in an aquarium until the adult emerges. The smaller nymphs take from 1 to 3 years to reach adulthood and that would be a long time to care for a pet as hungry as a dragonfly. A dragonfly's diet consists mainly of insects; so, if you are keeping one in an aquarium, you need a constant supply of live food. You cannot keep more than one nymph in your aquarium—at least, not for long.

Your aquarium can just be a jar with a layer of sand and stones on the bottom, and a water plant. Use pond water, and keep the jar in a cool place. Remember, if the water gets warm, the oxygen will be driven off and the nymph will drown from lack of air.

The aquarium can serve as a laboratory for studying dragonfly behavior. You might, for example, try to find out which pond creatures the dragonfly nymph prefers to eat. Count out several mayflies, mosquitoes, or whatever insects are common in the pond where you do your collecting. Does one kind of insect get eaten first because it is more easily seen, or is it all a question of luck?

You could find out if putting water plants in the aquarium helps the hunter or the hunted. Do the prey animals take cover among the plants? See how long it takes a dragonfly nymph to catch five mosquito larvae in a jar of water. Compare this to a dragonfly in a jar with water and a plant.

It is also interesting to notice what part of the aquarium the dragonfly prefers. Does it rest on a plant or stone? Does it have a favorite place or does it wander about? Does it wait for its prey to come to it or does it give chase?

Another question you could try to answer is: How big a dinner will a hungry dragonfly eat? Can it eat a tadpole or a small fish? How close is the prey before the nymph attacks? Can you "fool" the nymph into attacking a little piece of dark paper?

Notice any changes that occur with a molt. Look

for changes in color and in the proportions of the body. Watch for the appearance of the wing pads.

You can also collect damselfly nymphs for your aquarium.

We have already said that you can recognize the slender damselfly nymph by its three flat tails which are gills. Sometimes, you find these fragile gills are broken. In most cases, the damselfly can get along for a time with the broken gills. So the gills cannot be completely responsible for breathing. Notice what happens to the broken gills at the next molt.

If you can find a nymph ready for its final molt, then you can witness one of the most spectacular sights of nature. It stops feeding for a few days and then crawls up on a weed or twig out of the water. The skin splits down the back and the dragonfly squirms and wriggles; finally, it pulls its long body out of the cast skin. Its wings stiffen and gradually the body takes on its bright, metallic color. The insect is ready to become the acrobat of the air for a few short weeks.

CHAPTER 13

The Case of the Caddisfly

SOMETIMES, when you are looking down into a stream or pond, you may see a little cluster of stones walking around. This will probably be the larva of the caddisfly, an unusual insect that is worth getting to know better.

The adult is rather like a small, drab moth. It flies mostly at night and, when resting, folds its wings tentlike over its body. Caddisflies are related to moths but belong to a separate order of insects. The name of the order is *Trichoptera* which means "hairy wing." Moths' wings are covered with tiny scales.

Some species of caddisflies become pests because of their great numbers. Hundreds of thousands emerge from the rivers and cluster so thickly around street lights that they block out the light. Mostly, they live for a few weeks on a diet of nectar. Their tongues are not coiled like those of butterflies and moths so they lap the nectar from flowers.

The female caddisflies lay their eggs in a stream or pond. However, there is one kind that attaches its

132 • EXPLORING THE INSECT WORLD

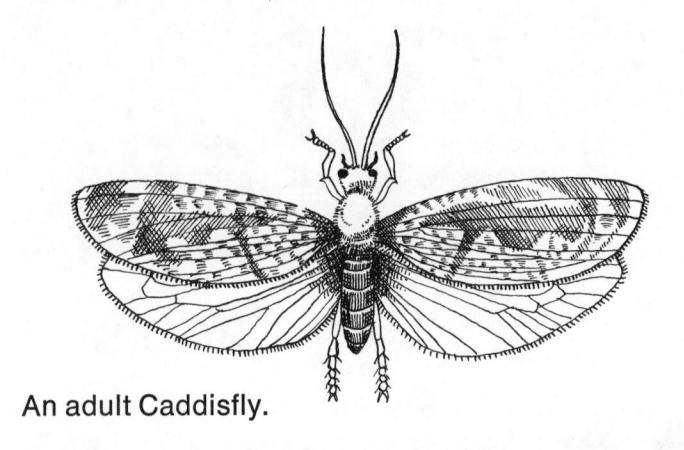

An adult Caddisfly.

eggs to tree twigs high above the water. Falling rains wash the larvae into the stream where they continue to develop. Another kind swims down into the water and lays its eggs on a submerged plant.

The caddisfly larva is a small caterpillarlike creature which must face the host of hungry enemies that you are beginning to recognize in the underwater world. Dragonfly nymphs lurk in the weeds, water scorpions hang with their breathing tubes extended

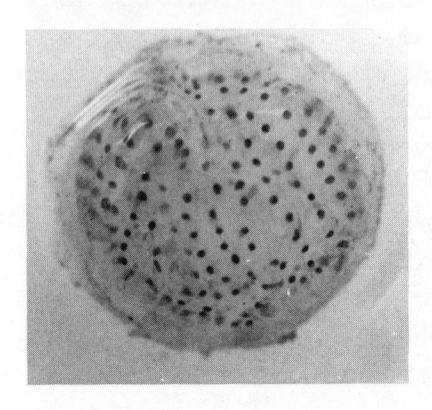

Caddis egg mass.

THE CASE OF THE CADDISFLY • *133*

to the surface and their grasping forelegs ready, and a water tiger attacks, as bloodthirsty as its namesake in the jungle.

So the little larva begins to collect material which it cements around its body, making itself a protective case. The type of case varies with the caddisfly—some cases are made of particles of sand and stone, others of sticks and leaves. As a rule, the heavier cases belong to caddisflies that live in fast-moving water. Caddisflies that live in still water have cases light enough to allow them to move freely. There are some kinds that make no cases at all.

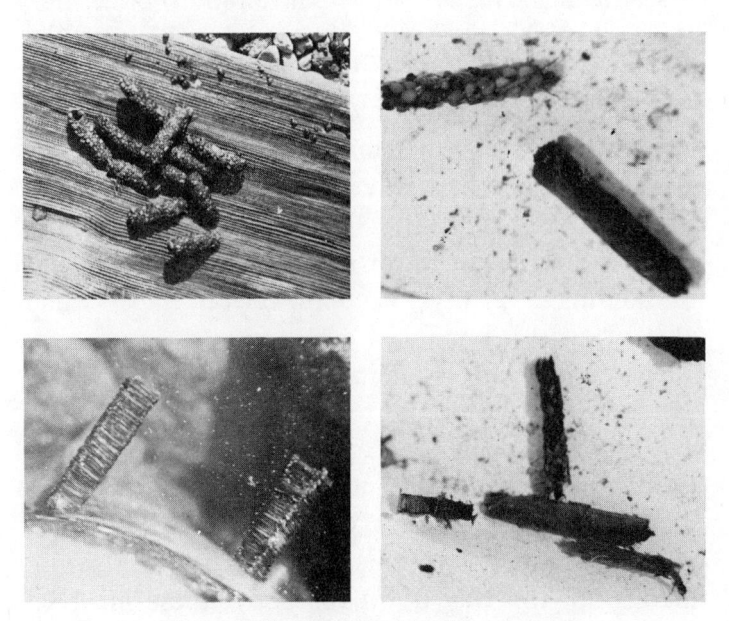

Four different Caddisfly cases.

Some cases are very unusual. Look for the snail-shell caddis. It is very tiny—about ⅛ inch across. The case is coiled like a snail shell. The chimney-case caddis builds a very neat case of plant material. It is square in cross section and tapers toward the tail end. Several kinds of caddisflies build tiny "log cabins" of twigs, pine needles, or grass stems. The larva cuts the material to the proper length with its jaws and then cements the pieces in place, crosswise, to the case.

Inside the case

Once you have found a caddisfly larva, watch it closely as it moves about. The head and thorax stick right out of the case as it creeps about. Pick up the case and gently try to pull the insect out. You will find that it has a good hold in there. In fact, if you keep pulling, you may damage the larva before it lets go the case. The best way to get it out is to slit the case open very carefully. Then you will see that the caddisfly has a pair of strong hooks at its hind end for holding it firmly (keep the insect moist while you work with it).

The caddis case is made of a lining of silk (from glands inside the insect) to which the stones, twigs, or leaves are added. The case is a tube with a large opening at the head end and a smaller opening at the other end. This allows the water to flow through the case. The larva has gills, similar to little white threads, all the way down the body; these must be bathed in water for the insect to breathe.

Caddisfly larva without case.

To see this movement of water through the case, put a larva in an open jar of water. Then put a drop of food-coloring liquid in front of the head end and you will be able to see the colored water drawn into the case.

Collecting and keeping caddis larvae
A good way to get to know the adult caddisflies is to raise them from larvae. This also gives you a chance to learn something of their lives.

When you collect caddis larvae, notice the conditions in which they live in the wild. Does the insect live in a pond or stream? What is the temperature of the water? What sort of food supply is available?

What materials are used for its case? Is it resting on weeds or gravel?

When bringing home the live caddis larvae, put them in a plastic bag of damp moss or waterweed and keep them cool. Do not carry them in a jar of water or they will die for lack of oxygen.

At home, you should try to duplicate the natural home of the caddisflies. Keep them in an aquarium, in pans, or in widemouthed jars. As has been mentioned before, the two most likely causes of trouble are the water temperature and lack of oxygen. You have to keep the water cool, near the temperature of the stream or pond. Perhaps there is a corner in the basement or in the shade where you can keep the larvae.

If your larvae are from a pond, they do not need as much oxygen as the ones that live in swift water. This is because there is more air trapped in the rippling water of a stream than in the calm waters of a pond. There are ways of getting more air into the water for your caddisflies. The best way is to use a "bubbler," such as the ones used in fish tanks. You can also increase the air supply by using a shallow pan which allows a wide surface of the water to be in contact with the air.

If you cannot use pond or stream water, then let tap water stand uncovered overnight or longer. This allows chlorine in the water to escape as a gas.

Most caddis larvae are plant eaters. Many live on decaying plant material. Put some algae-covered stones, some waterweed, and dead leaves into your pan and find out what your species of caddisfly prefer.

The ways of a caddisfly

When you have your "rearing pans" set up, you will be able to make some observations on growth and behavior. The caddisfly molts inside its case, usually pushing the old skin out the front or back opening. It has, of course, to add to its case as it grows.

If you work carefully with a blunt probe—a toothpick—at the hind end of the larva, you can chase it out of its case without damaging either the animal or its case. You will find that the larva recognizes its case and returns to it. What happens if you offer it several empty cases, including its own?

Leave a larva, without a case, in water with a fresh supply of building materials and it will make a new case. How long does it take? Some make a quick, rough case and then improve on it for the next day or so. Can you get the larva to include tiny beads, pieces of broken shells, or fragments of glass in the construction of an extra-fancy case?

What is the result if you give a stone-case builder only plant material? Or if you give only sand to a species that usually uses pine needles? Will they try to use a new type of material, or will they remain naked?

If all goes well in your aquarium, the larva will become a pupa, the stage during which it makes ready to become a flying adult. The pupating larva fixes itself to some object in the water such as a plant or stone. It then forms a silk screen across both ends of its case, sometimes adding a stone lid. There is still a flow of water through the case, but it is hard for enemies to get at the pupa. Some kinds of caddisflies leave the water altogether to pupate and are found in damp ground close to the stream or pond. This stage varies in length. Some species spend the whole summer as pupae, but most emerge as adults in 2 or 3 weeks.

Once you have pupae in your pans, you should cover them. An old nylon stocking stretched over the pan makes a good cover. It would be a pity if the adult were to emerge and fly off without your ever getting a chance to see it!

Back at the stream

Remember that an insect reared in the captivity of a jar may not behave exactly as it would in the wild. So it is important to make observations in nature. How much protection does the case provide? How does a predator attack a caddisfly? (This is a question you might investigate in your aquarium too.)

While you are exploring the stream, you may meet a very surprising caddisfly. This caddis spins a silk net underwater, attaching it to rocks or logs so that the current flows through the net. This mesh net, or seine, is very like a fisherman's net and, when you remember that the caddis weaves it underwater in the swift current, it is most remarkable.

Beside the net is the caddisfly's dwelling tube

where the caddis waits for its dinner to be caught. Most of these caddises will eat any small bits of plant or animal material caught in the net.

The seine builders will not make their nets in the still waters of an aquarium. Nor can you examine the net out of water—it just becomes a shapeless tangle. So, if you are going to get to know this caddis, you will have to put on your rubber boots and go exploring the streams. Good luck!

CHAPTER 14

Man's Insect Enemies

ONE INSECT does not do much damage by itself. But millions of insects can.

The most frightening and spectacular destruction occurs when the locust, a relative of the grasshopper, swarms, leaving a path of devastation and famine.

Do you remember Laura Ingalls Wilder's account of the "glittering cloud" of grasshoppers when she lived on the Banks of Plum Creek?

The cloud was hailing grasshoppers. The cloud was grasshoppers. Their bodies hid the sun and made darkness. Their thin, large wings gleamed and glittered. The rasping whirring of their wings filled the whole air and they hit the ground and the house with the noise of a hailstorm....

... Grasshoppers beat down from the sky and swarmed thick over the ground. Their long wings were folded and their strong legs took them hopping everywhere. The air whirred and the roof went on sounding like a roof in a hailstorm.

MAN'S INSECT ENEMIES • *141*

Then Laura heard another sound, one big sound made of tiny nips and snips and gnawings.

"The wheat!" Pa shouted. He dashed out the back door and ran toward the wheat-field.[1]

The grasshoppers ate the wheat field and the whole prairie bare. There was no crop, and no feed for the cows and horses. The grasshoppers brought hard times to the pioneer family.

The Bible tells of plagues of locusts thousands of years ago; even now, these plagues bring famine to the warm countries of Africa and the Middle East.

The story of the fight against locusts is a good example of how important it is to know all about the insect that you want to control. Scientists were puzzled because swarms of locusts seemed to appear from nowhere. There was no gradual build-up of numbers. Quite suddenly, millions of locusts would be on the move.

The answer to the sudden appearance of the locusts is that these insects lead a double life. They can live for generations as a large green grasshopper feeding mainly on grasses. This is called the *solitary phase*. Then one year, there may be an especially good breeding season, or the breeding area may be small and the eggs crowded. Great numbers of little hoppers hatch. They change in appearance and behavior. This is the *gregarious phase*. The hoppers are

[1] From "The Glittering Cloud" in ON THE BANKS OF PLUM CREEK by Laura Ingalls Wilder. Text copyright 1937 by Laura Ingalls Wilder. Copyright renewed 1965 by Roger L. MacBride. By permission of Harper & Row, Publishers, Inc.

brightly colored and lively and hungry. It is almost as if they had joined an army, donned bright uniforms, and set off to conquer the world.

The locust army marches across the land—eating, molting, and growing. When they become full-grown, they develop wings and take to the air. The swarms travel right across countries.

Control of the locust swarms had to become an international project. The Anti-Locust Research Centre was set up in London, England.

The Centre collects reports from the locust areas of the world and the scientists can forecast when swarms may start and where they will move. Then the insects can be attacked with sprays and the crops protected.

The scientists also try to find out more about the insects. They study how they react to changes in temperature, humidity and light. They can make them change from the solitary to the gregarious phase in the laboratory. To win the war against the locust, the scientist must understand the enemy. Insecticide, even tons of it, is only part of the answer.

Other hungry pests

Many of the insects we looked at in Chapter 5—the insects that eat plants—have an important place in recycling plant materials. They eat leaves and dead and dying wood. But they eat the food we want for ourselves and destroy the timber we want for our houses, so they become our insect enemies.

Often, it is our own fault that an insect becomes a

MAN'S INSECT ENEMIES • *143*

pest. We have upset the balance of nature by providing the right conditions for a population explosion

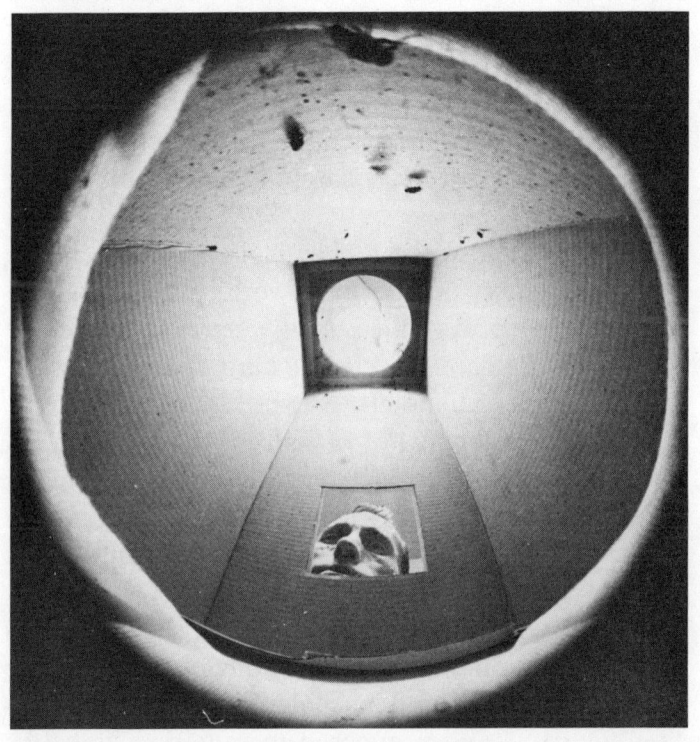

Male screwworm flies being exposed to radiation at Mission, Texas. During the sterilization process, canisters containing 30,000 flies are exposed to Cobalt 60 radiation sources at the rearing facility. From each canister 15 pupae are removed, hatched and mated with fertile females to check for fertility. This test guarantees the effectiveness of the sterilization process. The sterile flies are then released.

of that particular type of insect. For example, a field of cabbages provides an unlimited supply for the cabbage white butterfly caterpillar. We cannot afford to grow cabbages for caterpillars so we kill them with chemical sprays. Then the poisonous sprays upset the balance still more by killing the enemies of the pest insect. There is a little parasitic wasp that kills many caterpillars each year. The poison spray kills this insect friend as surely as it kills our insect enemies.

We cannot do without chemical sprays. There are too many hungry people in the world. But we do need to find safe sprays and *selective* sprays. These are chemicals that are directed toward the pest insect, and not against all insects.

There are other ways of fighting insects, too. In the next chapter, we will find that we have many allies in the insect world that can help control the pests. Scientists have even learned to use insect diseases to kill insects. Imagine a fly with flu!

Another method that has been used successfully is to sterilize the males. This was done on a large scale on screwworm flies. The males—millions and millions of them—were exposed to radiation and then released. They were infertile but otherwise unharmed. These males mated with females. The females laid eggs but the eggs could not hatch. No young screwworms from these eggs would find their way into cuts on the skin of livestock and weaken or kill the animals.

Insects that talk with chemicals

Chapter 10 tells you how to lay an ant trail. If you try this you are finding out about *pheromones*. Pheromones are chemicals which insects use to give each other information. For example, the ant leaves a scent trail to tell other ants where they can find food.

One of the first of these chemical pheromones to be studied was the "queen substance" that comes from the queen bee. The worker bees constantly lick the queen. They receive some queen substance which is then passed on from worker to worker through the exchange of food. As long as the workers are receiving traces of this pheromone, they know that all is well with the queen. If the queen is removed from the hive, they quickly know it and begin building large queen cells to rear new queens.

Female moths give off a pheromone which can attract the males from long distances. By studying pheromones, scientists hope to find ways of attracting and trapping one specific pest insect. This idea has already been used in the control of wasps. An attractant is mixed with a poison. The chemicals are combined in a plastic material so that the chemicals are given off slowly. Only wasps come to the bait and are killed. Helpful insects, like bees, ignore it.

Malaria

Another insect that has had a great effect on man is the mosquito. The female mosquito needs a meal of blood before she lays her eggs. Her bite can make you itch, but a more serious consequence is that, in some parts of the world, mosquitoes carry malaria parasites. These infected mosquitoes spread the disease to man.

To prevent malaria, we must control mosquitoes. To control mosquitoes, we need to know their habits.

In Chapter 11 we found that mosquito larvae live in the still water of ponds. They breathe at the surface. Scientists have used this fact in mosquito control. They can drown the larvae by spreading a thin film of oil over the water's surface.

Another way of cutting down the mosquito population is to clear away the plants around the water's edge where the mosquitoes hide from predators. Still another way is draining stagnant pools and marshes. This cuts down on breeding places.

The discovery of DDT provided a quick answer to the mosquito problem. It had a great impact on the mosquito and, also, on man. Malaria almost disappeared. Human populations increased rapidly, and this has brought its own problems. Now we find that the effects of DDT go far beyond killing insect pests. Birds lay eggs that cannot hatch and fish accumulate the poison in their bodies.

New strains of mosquitoes have developed which can resist the sprays. At the same time, man has become less resistant to the disease. A new outbreak of malaria now would have disastrous results.

So we must find another answer. Perhaps, it will be by finding an immunization against the malaria parasites. In the meantime, the scientists are, again, studying the habits of the mosquito in an attempt to win the war against insects and disease. Always, the best defense lies in knowing the enemy.

CHAPTER 15

Man's Insect Friends

MAN MAKES USE of insects in a variety of ways. Termites and locusts are used as food by some primitive peoples. Manna, eaten by Moses and the tribes of Israel, was provided by scale insects. The bright wings of beetles and butterflies are used for decoration, and crickets are kept in little cages by the Chinese to provide music.

Many dyes come from insects—red cochineal from scale insects and indelible ink from galls. The Chinese have reared silk moths for thousands of years. They unwind the fine silk strands from the cocoon and spin it into beautiful cloth. Man-made dyes and fabrics have made these uses less important.

Insects have occasionally been used in medicine. Some Indian tribes use ants with powerful jaws to hold together a gaping wound. It has been found that some kinds of maggots help open sores heal more quickly. You can see why these remedies are not used in modern medicine.

Modern science, on the other hand, has many needs for insects. One of the most important of these is in genetics, the study of how characteristics are passed from parent to child. The little fruit fly, *Drosophila,* has helped answer many puzzles. This fly has red eyes, straight bristles, and long wings. In laboratories, there are colonies of flies with white eyes, or twisted bristles, or short wings. By crossbreeding, scientists learn how characteristics are passed to the next generation. All these strange little creatures have added a little bit to our knowledge about ourselves.

Pollination

Most people would say that the honeybee is man's best insect friend. This is true, not just because it makes honey and wax, but because of its role in pollination. Some farmers pay beekeepers to bring their

An unusual road sign in Oregon where farmers "domesticate" the alkali bee to increase pollination.

hives into the orchards when the trees are in bloom.

Farmers in Oregon have tried a new approach to encourage bees to pollinate their alfalfa crops. They provide homes for wild bees. These are the solitary bees that are mentioned in Chapter 9. They do not give honey, but they are good pollinators.

The first bees the farmers used were *alkali* bees, which have their burrows in soil that is *alkaline,* or "salty." By copying the soil conditions that the bees like, the farmers made artificial "bee beds." It was found that more bees meant more seed.

Boards drilled with holes provide nesting sites for hundreds of leaf-cutter bees.

The beds cannot be used everywhere, so some farmers make homes for a small leaf-cutting bee that lives in holes in wood. The farmers use boards drilled with hundreds of holes to provide nesting sites for the bees. Some shelters are quite elaborate. In the high country, where the nights get cold, farmers put a heating coil in the roof of the shelter to keep the bees warm at night. The adult bees sleep in the holes and, with "central heating," they get to work earlier in the morning!

Although the bees are solitary, they do not mind living in holes close to each other. But if the nesting sites are *too* big, then a bee has trouble remembering its own home. The bee finds its hole by recognizing "landmarks" around it. We know that bees can see different colors, so painting sections of the boards with contrasting colors helps the bees find their own holes.

In the last chapter, we found that scientists must "know their enemy." They also need to "know their friend."

The food chain

Another useful aspect of insect life which is often overlooked, especially when the insects are eating our crops, is that they are an important link in the food chain. If an insect lays 200 eggs, only two of these need become adults to keep the numbers of that kind of insect level. The other 198 eggs and larvae are available as food for other animals.

You might think there are some insects that we could well do without, but the variety of large animals in the world depends on the variety of small creatures. That is what ecology is all about. A robin cannot live on dead leaves, but it *can* live on the insects and worms that live on dead leaves.

Biological control

An exciting answer to some insect problems is to enlist the help of the "good" insects to eat up the "bad" insects. This is called biological control.

The idea is not new. If you keep a cat to scare away mice, you are using biological control. Snails eating the green algae in an aquarium is an example of an animal controlling a plant.

Quite a number of our insect pests came from other countries. They may not even have been recognized as pests in the original country. They are introduced here by accident and, without any of their natural enemies, their numbers grow rapidly.

Over 100 years ago, some acacia trees were brought from Australia to California. On these trees were some tiny, sap-sucking insects called cottony-cushion scales. They thrived in the new country and soon spread to orange trees and other trees. The leaves of the orange trees looked like cottony cushions, and the trees began to die. The growers were in despair.

The Department of Agriculture sent an entomologist to Australia to find out what kept the scale insects in check there. The answer was the vedalia beetle, a little ladybird.

Vedalia beetles were sent to California. An infested tree was covered with a cloth tent and 139 of the beetles were released. They ate and ate and produced more beetles. Soon there were enough beetles to turn loose in the orchards, and these beetles ate and ate and produced more beetles. Within 2 years, the outbreak of cottony-cushion scale was controlled, and the orange groves were saved.

Insect "weed killers"

Many of the plant-eating insects are pests, but there are cases when they are our friends. This happens when the plant they are eating is a pest.

In the western states, there is a yellow weed called tansy ragwort. It crowds out grass and other plants in the pasture. It causes a fatal liver disease in cattle and horses. Even dried in hay, it can kill cattle.

The farmers wanted rid of tansy ragwort, and they turned to the entomologists for help. Was there anything that would attack the weed? Europe is the native home of tansy ragwort so the search for an insect was centered in France. The most promising insect seemed to be the cinnabar moth. Its yellow and black caterpillars eat ragwort leaves and flowers.

The scientists had to be careful that the insects brought into this country were free from parasites and disease. They had to make sure that the cinnabar moth ate only tansy ragwort and would not become a pest itself.

One thousand moths were released in Oregon but, in following years, no caterpillars or moths were to be found. What had gone wrong? There was certainly plenty of food.

Perhaps too few moths had been released. They

154 • EXPLORING THE INSECT WORLD

Cinnabar moth caterpillars eating tansy ragwort.

might have become too scattered to find mates and reproduce. But there was another worry. Were the caterpillars being eaten by birds?

In France, there is a yellow and black caterpillar that is poisonous to birds. So the French birds leave *all* yellow and black caterpillars alone—even harmless ones. Would Oregon birds do the same?

More moths were released and, this time, the population began to build up. The caterpillars were safe from birds and seemed to be suited to life in the

Close-up of a cinnabar moth caterpillar eating a tansy ragwort.

western states. But there is still a lot of ragwort, so let us hope that new, hungry generations of caterpillars and moths are ready to weed the state.

Insects everywhere

We have found insects everywhere. Some compete with us and some help us. This is their world as well as ours.

No book could be big enough to tell you *all* about insects. You must go and discover their world yourself.

Bibliography

Hutchins, Ross E. CADDIS INSECTS. New York: Dodd, Mead & Company, 1966.

Jaques, H. E. HOW TO KNOW INSECTS. Dubuque, Iowa: William C. Brown Company, 1947.

Lutz, Frank E. FIELD BOOK OF INSECTS. New York: G. P. Putnam's Sons, 1948.

Mitchell, Robert T. and Zim, Herbert. BUTTERFLIES AND MOTHS. New York: Golden Press, 1964.

Shuttlesworth, Dorothy. THE STORY OF ANTS. New York: Doubleday & Company, Inc., 1964.

Simon, Hilda. DRAGONFLIES. New York: The Viking Press, Inc., 1972.

Zim, Herbert and Cottam, Clarence. INSECTS. New York: Golden Press, 1956.

Index

abdomen, structure of, 24–26
antennae, 18
anther, 38
Anti-Locust Research Centre (London), 142
ants and ant-watching, 35, 98–105
   soldier, 12
anus, 24
aphids, 82–84
aquarium, 119–20, 129–30, 137–38
arthropods, 11
armor, insect, 11–12
assembling, 35–36
attracting insects, 26–35
   See also capturing and collecting

bees and bee-watching, 89–92, 149–51
  dances, 88–89
  and pollination, 39–40
  solitary, 93–96
beetles, 21, 40–42
  "undertaker," 7
behavior, territorial, 122
blood, 26
bottom dwellers, 117–19
brain, 26
breathing, 13–14

builders, city, 98–110
butterflies, 42–44

caddisfly, 131–39
capturing and collecting insects, 27–31, 33–34, 35, 135–36
carabid, 78
case, caddis, 133–37
caterpillars
  keeping, 50–53
  silk-spinning, 75–76
Cecropia moth, 70–71
chitin, 12
cinnabar moth, 153–54
citrus industry, 7, 152–53
city builders, 98–110
click beetle, 56–57
Coleoptera, 42
collecting insects. *See* capturing and collecting
collection, gall, 62–63
commuters, surface, 116–17
control, biological, 152–53
cottony-cushion scale, 152–53

damselfly, 121–30
DDT, 146
Department of Agriculture (U.S.), 152
destruction by insects, 140–44
digestive system, 25

Diptera, 40
dissection, 25
dragonfly, 121–30
driver ant, 101
Drosophila, 149
dyes, 148

earwig, 85–86
enemy, insects as man's, 140–47
entomologist, definition and work, 7–8
exoskeleton, 11–12, 14, 15, 16
exploring a pond, 111–20
eye, compound, 19

Fabre, Jean Henri, 75–76, 95, 96
fall webworm, 74
femur, 56
firefly, 33–34
fly, 23, 40–42
flying, 21–24
food, insects as man's, 148
food chain, 151–52
fossils, 10
friend, insects as man's, 148–55

galls, plant, 59–70
ganglia, 26
garbage disposals, 85–86
genetics, 149
goldenrod galls, 64
grasshoppers, 41, 54–56
ground beetle, 78–79
growth of insects, 14–16

head, structure of, 18–19
hearing, 18

heart, 8, 25, 26
hemoglobin, 26, 118
homes, insects, 59–70
house builders, 87–97
hover fly, 40–41, 83
Hymenoptera, 39

ichneumen wasp, 84
inquilines, 63
insects
  beginnings, 9–11
  capturing, 27–31, 33–34, 35, 135–36
  for biological control, 152–53
  definition and features, 11–12
  destruction by, 140–44
  and the food chain, 151–52
  as food for man, 148
  growth, 14–17
  and man, 140–55
  pond, 111–38
  social, 87–92, 98–110
  structure, 12–13, 18–26
  water, 111–38
  as weed killers, 153–55
insecticides, 143–44, 146–47

jaw, structure of, 12

labium, 19
labrum, 19
ladybird, 82–84
larva, 16
legs, structure of, 20
Lepidoptera, 42–43
light, attraction to, 27–31
lights, colored, 30–31

light trap, 29–30
locust, 141–42

malaria, 145–57
Malpighian tubes, 25
mandible, 19
manna, 148
maxillae, 19
mayflies, 117–19
metamorphosis, 16
midges, 48
molting, 53
mosquitoes, 145–47
moths, 35–36, 42–44, 50
mouth, structure of, 19
mummies, 84

nervous system, 18
nests
   ant, 105–110
   artificial, 96–97

oak apples, 59, 68–69
ocelli, 19
Odonata, 20
On the Banks of Plum Creek (Wilder), 141
ovaries, 38
ovipositor, 84

parasites, 84–85
parasol ants, 102
Pemphigus galls, 66–68
phases, solitary and gregarious, 141
pheromones, 145
phototactism
   negative, 35
   positive, 27

pistil, 38
pitcher plant, 47–48
pitfall trap, 78–79
plants
   that eat insects, 46–48
   eaten by insects, 49–58
   as homes for insects, 59–70
   and pollination, 38–46, 149–51
   structure of, 38
pollen, 38
pollination, 38–46, 149–51
pond insects, 111–20
praying mantis, 79–82
predators, 77–84
pronuba, 44
pupa, 16, 17

queen
   ant, 99–100
   bee, 87

repletes, 101
root feeders, 56–57

sense organs, 18
setae, 24
sex organs, 25
silkworm, 70
smell, sense of, 18
Snodgrass, R. E., 72, 73
soldier ants, 12
solitary bees and wasps, 93–96
sounds, insect, 36
species, insect, 7
Sphex wasp, 95, 96
spiders, 70–71
spinners, 70–76
spiracles, 14

sprays, poisonous, 143–44
stamen, 38
sterilization of insects, 144
stereotaxis, 85
stick insects, 20–21
stigma, 38
stomach, 25
surface
  commuters, 116–17
  dwellers, 112–14
sugaring, 34–35
sundew, 46

tansy ragwort, 153–54
taste, sense of, 18
tent caterpillars, 71–74
termites, 58
terrarium, 48
thigmotaxis, 85
thorax, structure of, 20–21

trachea, 14, 25
Trichoptera, 131

vedalia beetles, 152–53
Venus fly-trap, 46–47
von Frisch, Karl, 88

wasps, 92–93
  solitary, 93–96
water beetles, 117
water insects, 20, 111–38
water striders, 112–14
water surface insects, 112–14
weaver ants, 102
weed killers, insects as, 152–53
Wilder, Laura Ingalls, 140
wing, structure of, 21–24
wireworm, 56–57
wrigglers, 114–15